SPUR PUBLICATIONS

FIELD SPORTS LIBRARY

HILL SHOOTING
AND
UPLAND GAMEKEEPING

Other Books by Guy N. Smith

*Gamekeeping and Shooting
for Amateurs*

Tobacco Culture—A D.I.Y. Guide

*Ferreting and Trapping for
Amateur Gamekeepers*

Hill Shooting
and
Upland Gamekeeping

by

GUY N. SMITH

DRAWINGS BY BOB SANDERS AND
ANTHEA HADLEY

Published by: SPUR PUBLICATIONS
SAIGA PUBLISHING CO LTD
1 ROYAL PARADE
HINDHEAD, SURREY GU26 6TD, ENGLAND

Photoset by Petaprint, Petersfield
Printed and bound by The Chapel River Press, Andover, Hants

Published by
SPUR PUBLICATIONS
SAIGA PUBLISHING CO. LTD.,
1 ROYAL PARADE, HINDHEAD, SURREY

Dedication

This book is dedicated to the hill-farmers,
the men who live with the wind in their teeth.

Acknowledgements

I acknowledge with thanks the assistance given by friends and colleagues. In particular, Bob Sanders and Anthea Hadley, for supplying many of the drawings. Lance Smith provided some of the photos.

Black Hill,
Clun.

Guy N. Smith

Contents

Monotone Illustrations

Illustrations in Colour

This One Did Not Escape: The fox, scourge of hill-farmers and game-preservers alike.

Introduction

Shooting in the hills has a unique appeal to the sportsman. In its own way it combines every aspect of the sport from the excitement of wildfowling whilst waiting at some secluded, possibly insignificant-looking pool, for duck to flight in at dusk, to the steep, sometimes treacherous ascent in quest of ptarmigan. No two areas are alike yet they have a common factor—unpredictability. Whilst in lowland areas the sportsman has an idea of what type of quarry to expect, this does not apply in the hills. On a day when conditions appear to be ideal, he may well return home with clean barrels, yet the following foray, in driving rain or enshrouding low cloud could yield the unexpected.

This type of shooting requires *dedication*. The one who is accustomed to regular moderate bags will soon tire of the effort necessary to produce a few rabbits or pigeons, perhaps nothing at all, and faced with a long drive home afterwards.

Yet the quality of sport is often far greater than that to be found on lower ground. A shot taken on a rugged hillside, where conventional stance and footwork is entirely out of the question, is doubly satisfactory. Surrounded by panoramic scenery, one is filled wirh a sense of truly being 'away from it all'. The odds are stacked against the upland gamekeeper, and the 'mewing' of a circling buzzard or the 'cronking' of a raven are a constant reminder that up in these hills Nature plays a greater part than Man.

The terrain itself has defied the march of progress, with the exception of the thousands of acres of Forestry Commission plantations. Even in an over-populated island such as ours, these hills must remain remote.

The object of this book is not simply to instruct the sportsman in the management of any acreage of such land which he may be fortunate enough to acquire. It is also an endeavour to portray a way of life, both that of the hardy hill-folk who live constantly with the wind in their teeth, and the birds and beasts which abound in this last stronghold, far

1

removed from the spreading tentacles of a nation where industry and commerce have taken over.

Above all, it is an appreciation on the part of the author after fifteen years of shooting and conservation in the Shropshire/Welsh border-hills, and no apologies are made for the many anecdotes contained within these pages. Each one serves to illustrate the mode of life and the sheer magnificence of this and many other similar tracts of hill country which would otherwise be ignored by the shooting man. Rents are normally low for such shoots where it is assumed that the game will be sparse. Success rests with the individual. Many leases are never renewed, and one often sees such shooting rights being offered in the press. The majority of the former tenants have lacked those qualities which are essential to a hill-shooter, determination and appreciation, and the measure of success or failure can only be determined by oneself.

CHAPTER 1

Establishing a Shoot

TYPES OF SHOOT

UPLAND OR LOWLAND?

From a sporting angle the two types of terrain are in direct contrast. Only the shooting man himself can decide which is more acceptable to nim, and his choice may be governed either by economic factors or preference for a particular kind of sport.

LOWLAND

This is 'conventional' shooting land and may consist either of arable or woodland. Generally it is more acceptable to game. Partridges prefer lower ground with root-crops for cover, and where rearing is practised it is far easier to hold birds within one's own boundaries.

With the break-up of the large estates, a sad factor which commenced after the last war, most of the shooting is leased to syndicates. Rents are rising annually, beyond the reach of the lone shooter, together with the cost of rearing-equipment, feedstuffs, gamekeeping requisites, and keepers' wages. In effect, the syndicate, the pooling of resources, is the only answer to maintaining a rural way of life, in any semblance of pre-war years. The cost of a gun in a syndicate varies from around £100 for rough-shooting to upwards of £1,000 where a professional gamekeeper rears the birds.

Even then one is restricted to a limited number of shooting days per season, and in many cases there will be no opportunity to shoot pigeons or vermin during the close season.

For the enthusiast, the man of moderate means who prefers to build-up his own shoot and enjoy the satisfaction of knowing that a successful season is entirely the result of his own work, he must search for somewhere cheaper, a place where there is freedom to experiment

3

and learn the ways of the wild. In most cases he will find this in upland regions.

UPLAND

The terrain will be either grazing land or forestry, or perhaps a mixture of both. It is not conducive to game, but the challenge will be all the greater. Possibly in the early stages a sportsman will have to be content with rabbits and pigeons alone, yet there will be ample vermin to be controlled, and the purpose of this book is to instruct the amateur in how to build-up his shoot. He will in no way equal his lowland counterpart in the head of game on his shoot, but for the lone shooter there is a vast potential.

The outlay will be relatively small. Rent will be lower, and the only expenditure will be feed for pheasants and gamekeeping equipment such as traps and snares.

There will be few easy shots. Every pheasant will test reflexes and markmanship, one's foothold will invariably be insecure, and the elements will play a major part in every outing. Cheaper sport, certainly, and not losing out on quality. However, the amount saved in cash will have to be made up in *effort*. Nothing will be easy, but the reward should be greater personal satisfaction.

FORESTRY COMMISSION SHOOTS
NOWHERE TO SHOOT—A COMMON PROBLEM

The spring of 1963 saw me without the shooting rights over any land, whatsoever, a situation which I had not encountered since my schooldays. Up until this time I had had as much shooting as any one man is entitled to. Indeed, it was a problem to find the time to walk over all the land which I had at my disposal. Then, suddenly, everything seemed to go wrong.

The woodland at the rear of our house, which I shot in return for a few small keeping duties, was taken over by a sand and gravel firm, the directors of which at once relished the sporting rights there with great enthusiasm. My own small shoot, some ten miles away, changed hands due to the farmer's retirement, whilst, all in the same week, the owner of the ninety acres, over which my father shot, decided that he would like to come and retire to a cottage locally, and shoot his own land.

So there we were, mid-April, with nowhere to shoot, and a couple of broods of day-old pheasant chicks ordered for the following month! I had several farms where I could go and shoot pigeons whenever I pleased, but this is small consolation for one who enjoys planning for the season ahead, and looking after his land throughout the whole year. Consequently, noticing an advertisement in the pages of a sporting journal, I wrote to the Forestry Commission to seek their help.

A RAY OF HOPE

I received a reply during the next week, to the effect that one of their newly acquired tracts of land, close to Shrewsbury, with the unusual name of "Huglith", was open to tenders. The following weekend, therefore, found me touring the area in question, in the company of a beat-forrester in a Forestry Commission Land Rover.

It was a little gem of a place, there was no doubt about that. Situated on the Shrewsbury-Bishop's Castle road, it comprised approximately seventy acres of grassland, the greater part of which consisted of a steep hill like a miniature sugar-loaf mountain. This latter was dotted with scrub trees, silver birch, gorse, and a few patches of heather. Suitable only for grazing land, it was ideal for reafforestation, and, no doubt, the farmer was only too pleased to part with this otherwise useless piece of land.

However, it was the small pool, surrounded by reeds at the base of Huglith Hill, which intrigued me most. The water was crystal clear, as opposed to the majority of these kind of ponds which are apt to be brackish and stagnant. It was approximately 25 yards long by 15 yards wide, and nowhere did it appear to be deeper than eighteen inches. It was an ideal pool, perfectly situated, for mallard to flight-in-to in the evenings, when dusk turned to deep darkness. This water was fed by a natural stream, a 'dingle' which had trickled incessantly down the hillside from time immemorial, wending its way through grassy, spacious silver-birch wood, taking a winding route which eventually ended in the clear, sparkling pool.

The boundaries of Huglith were determined by a stout fence of 'rabbit-proof' netting, so widely used by the Forestry Commission in the British Isles. As a "pocket-handkerchief" shoot it had possibilities for the man who was content just to bag an odd pheasant, a brace if he was lucky, with the chance of a duck at evening flight. It was, indeed, a lone sportsman's delight, this strangely shaped hill with its beautiful surroundings.

So, in due course, I made my offer, and all I had to do now was to await a decision on the part of the landlords. The weeks passed, and my pheasant chicks on the lawn at home grew into poults, until, eventually, their release was the only answer to a particularly bad outbreak of feather-pecking. I was tempted to presume tenancy of Hughlith, and release them there, but I was reluctant to do so until the lease had been signed. Consequently, I sold them to a friend who had several hundred acres of shooting rights, to release along with his 300 six-week-old poults. My rearing efforts had been barely rewarded from a monetary aspect, and I would have to do without a small stock of pheasants on Huglith when my tenancy began.

The end of August finally arrived, and still I had received neither acceptance nor refusal of my offer for my intended shoot. I visited it once in the meantime, primarily to tip a bag of barley into the pool, for I wanted any duck which might already know about this wonderful little roost to begin using it before 1st September. It looked much the same as it had when I had last visited it, only the leaves on the silver-birch trees were already beginning to take on an autumnal colouring, and I was reminded that it was time that I pursued my tender, and asked for a decision. Up until now I had been reluctant to do so, not wishing to appear overeager, and pester those who were responsible for the country's afforestation plans.

DISAPPOINTMENT AND CONSOLATION

On 1st September, sensing that all was not well regarding my shooting rights, I telephoned my prospective landlords. There appeared to be some confusion over the whole business, and it was not until another three days had passed that the whole business was sorted out. It transpired that the previous owner of Huglith had not realised, when he sold that 70 acres to the Forestry Commission, that he was parting with the shooting rights! Consequently, as it is always the Commission's policy to favour shooting tenants or owners of land which they purchase, I was backing a loser from the start!

So, Huglith Hill slipped tantalisingly out of my grasp when it was all but mine. The Forestry Commission, who always try to be fair in such cases, came up with a "consolation" shoot, my present 600 acres in the

Shropshire/Welsh border hills. I have no regrets, for I have come to love this place dearly over the last fifteen years, but I often wonder what it would have been like shooting at Huglith, that miniature, country-lover's paradise.

So, Fate decreed that I was to come to the 'Black Hill', coincidentally only a few miles distant from my great-grandfather's birthplace!

Let us, though, examine these Forestry Commission shoots in greater detail, so that the prospective tenant may have a better idea of that which he is taking on before signing a lease, and then regretting his decision when he discovers that his acreage, large or small, is not a haven for game.

WHAT IS AVAILABLE?

The average sportsman is inclined to treat the idea of a Forestry Commission shoot as something of a 'white elephant'. The lure of a large acreage for a reasonably low rent might tempt him to investigate one of the advertisements which appear in rural periodicals comparatively frequently. An inspection of the sporting rights open to tender will at once disillusion him. Mostly, they consist of impenetrable conifer thickets, often on a steep hillside, interspersed with a network of rutted roads. Any idea which he might have had of organised shooting, however basic, at once evaporates. There is little space for more than two or three guns to walk the rides through these artificial forests, with a dog doing its utmost to pick up a scent on the thick carpet of pine-needles beneath the closely planted firs.

PERSEVERANCE

This is the picture which presents itself, but perseverance is necessary if the obvious situation is to be overcome, and some sport enjoyed in spite of the overwhelming odds against conventional shooting. I have rented 600 acres of such terrain for fifteen seasons now, and such has been my success that I have recently renewed my lease.

In return for your rent, you have the right to carry a gun over X acres of land. Nothing more. One must either be content to ramble round every now and then with the prospect of a shot at rabbit, pigeon, or vermin, or else set to work, and make the shoot something of an investment. I chose to do the latter, and perhaps this may serve as a guide to others who find themselves in my position—the choice between

7

1-1   Detecting Game: It is on the boundaries where sport will
be found.

(photo: Guy Smith)

a Forestry Commission lease or clay-pigeon shooting!

ATTRACTING GAME TO UNATTRACTIVE SURROUNDINGS

The centre of any conifer forest is virtually useless with regard to game prospects, either for roosting or breeding. The dark gloomy interior offers nothing in the way of food for pheasants, so it is on the boundaries where your sport will be found. Those pheasants which roost in the fringes of your fir wood will make for the adjoining fields at first light, returning at dusk. So, unless you are fortunate in being able to rent some adjoining arable or grazing, you must provide sufficient food within your own woods to tempt them to remain.

FEEDING

Hoppers, whilst serving a purpose, have two great drawbacks. The grain is too easily accessible, and the pheasant having filled his crop in a very short time will wander off for the rest of the day. Secondly, this food supply will quickly become known to vermin, and also to any local poachers. If you are not able to visit your shoot regularly in order to feed by hand, then situate your hopper in a clearing well away from the main rides, but make sure that dense undergrowth is not in close proximity, otherwise Reynard will soon catch on to the fact that if he lies quietly in wait he will be sure of an easy meal.

Hand feeding is always best, scattering the grain amongst the undergrowth so that the birds will have to *spend time* searching for it. The best results will be obtained this way, and if you are unable to visit your shoot daily, then perhaps a *reliable* farmer will help out in return for some shooting. Much as you rely on his fields, he is equally indebted to your woods for providing roosting for the pheasants. One is a complement to the other, and an alliance with the local farmers is invaluable.

VERMIN CONTROL

Where grain is being fed, vermin will follow. Grey squirrels are the scourge of any forest, and a system of tunnel-traps, *inspected daily,* is your only really successful means of waging war against this enemy. You will have to rely on the gun for controlling the corvine tribe, and I have found that they decoy better in thickly wooded country than anywhere else. One must take care, though, that the large black predator

9

gliding-in to answer your calling is not a raven. The raven is now breeding prolifically in many wooded, mountainous areas, and together with the buzzard, which you are also bound to come across, it is protected.

It is inadvisable to shoot near to feeding-points, even if you are only accounting for the odd carrion crow which rises at your approach. I prefer to have an intensified onslaught on vermin immediately after the shooting season is over, and then allow the woods a certain amount of peace during the nesting months.

REARING

Of course, in order to increase a very sparse stock of pheasants one must release a few hand-reared birds. Complex as this is on conventional lowland arable shoots, it is a hundred times more so in Forestry Commission thickets. Foxes will quickly prey on poults released in these dark barren woodlands, so your only chance is to turn your birds on to the fields of a friendly neighbouring farmer. After all, *his* birds have been roosting in your woods, so in effect you are repaying him for those which you have shot. Maybe he will even build, and look after, a release-pen for you.

DUCK

One item of sport which is usually over-looked in thickly afforested areas is *duck-flighting*. The Forestry Commission usually build artificial reservoirs in case of fire, but in most instances these are too deep to attract duck. However, sometimes a natural spring has been developed into a shallow pool, and it is here that your flighting prospects lie. I am adamant that such a pond, even if remote from a recognised flightline, will attract the odd duck from time to time.

I have a pool on my own shoot which is no more than fifteen yards long by ten yards wide with a depth of about a foot. It is surrounded by fir-thickets, and after I had fed it regularly for the whole of my first season, without so much as a preening feather to show for my efforts, I dismissed the idea of it ever becoming a flightpond. Then, towards the end of that February, mallard began to use it, and I have averaged about a dozen each successive season. Hardly an impressive bag, admittedly, but it represents many hours of pleasant anticipation, and after an otherwise blank day, there is always the chance of a shot at duck!

RABBITS AND PIGEONS

Naturally, rabbits and pigeons will form the nucleus of sport on the majority of Forestry Commission shoots. Pigeons are difficult to flight in large forests, but a study of wind direction will enable you to stand a chance at least. Find out the fields on which the flocks are feeding, bear in mind that they will fly *into* the wind when coming into roost, unless there is a conveniently placed valley for them to follow, and if you position yourself on the fringe of your *tallest* belt of trees, the chances are that you will get some shooting. Pigeons do not like roosting in young plantations. Decoys will be a waste of time, for as the pigeons leave the fields, their crops stuffed to bursting point with clover or wheat, they know exactly where they are going, and nothing will dissuade them from their favourite roost.

THERE IS ALWAYS POTENTIAL

The potential is there, in spite of a large tract of uninteresting manmade forest. With a little effort you can create some pheasant and duck-shooting, with rabbits and pigeons always available to supplement those days when there seems to be little else about. You will never shoot large bags on a Forestry Commission shoot, but, there again, what true sportsman wants to make a slaughter of it?

This is but a brief summary of that which you are likely to encounter on a shoot of this nature, and the majority of points will be dealt with in detail in later chapters of this book.

The following, though, is an account of my own efforts to increase my sport on the 'Black Hill', and it is my hope that readers will learn from the mistakes I made without having to endure the disappointments which befell me. Up until then, although I had had a fair amount of gamekeeping experience, it had all been conducted on *lowland* shoots. I was soon to learn that there was a vast difference between my previous duties on arable land and those in these beautiful border hills.

EARLY DAYS ON THE BLACK HILL

This new project of mine was regarded as an act of insanity by my shooting colleagues, for, with the same monetary outlay, I could have taken a gun in a first class shooting syndicate, being assured of sport, week after week, during the season. As it was, I was paying an annual rent for the privilege of travelling some 140 miles each weekend in order to walk over a tract of land which was virtually devoid of game.

However, I had not taken this irrevocable step (for I had signed a long lease to begin with) in order to participate in an aimless weekly outing with nothing to show for it. My newly acquired land presented me with a challenge, an incentive to make something out of nothing. I vowed, at the beginning, that I would attempt to build up, and maintain, a stock of resident game, not merely with a view to killing the fruits of my labours, but to enjoy the complete satisfaction of knowing that pheasants, rabbits, hares, and wild-duck abounded in these windswept mountain woodlands, solely on account of my own efforts at conservation.

A VERMIN KINGDOM

My first task was to reduce the vermin population, for foxes, grey squirrels, and the corvine tribe, had already claimed this particular area as their rightful kingdom. My assault on Reynard and his red brethren entailed much hard work, for it was necessary to be abroad just as day was breaking if one was to stand a chance of meeting up with this cunning enemy. Many times, during those early days, I started from home at 3 a.m. in order to be in my woodlands at dawn. Success was not easy, but it came, sure enough. At the end of the first twelve months of my lease, I had accounted for no fewer than 28 foxes, following this up with another 14 in the following year. Carrion crows, on the lookout for helpless new-born lambs, on the adjoining sheep fields, were regularly falling to my gun, as were their cousins, the magpie and the jay, those relentless hunters of game-birds' and songsters' eggs. With each one I shot, I had the satisfaction of knowing that I had probably saved a nest in the following spring.

EXPERIMENTING WITH PHEASANTS

Soon I realised that the numbers of the enemy were dwindling. I had no wish to exterminate them, merely wishing to strike a balance of nature. When I considered that I had achieved this target, as far as I was able to judge, I decided that it was now time to try and increase the number of pheasants, which, up until now, had been seen merely on isolated occasions on the edge of the woods. Consequently, I

1-2 Forestry Commission land: Artificial landscapes created for a purpose   (photo: Guy Smith)

concentrated my efforts on rearing a clutch of pheasant eggs under a broody hen on my lawn at home.

I was reasonably successful at the first attempt, and that August I released fifteen 6-week-old pheasant poults into the wild. The following year I turned out no fewer than thirty. The layman may be forgiven for thinking that I was carrying out the death-sentence by feeding them to the foxes which had escaped my previous onslaught. I had, in fact, already accustomed these young pheasants to roosting at night, above ground level, by means of fixing perches in their pen, prior to their release. With regard to providing them with a regular food supply, I installed a series of empty five-gallon oil drums, cleansed out, and perforated at the base in order to allow the grain to trickle through as the birds pecked at it, situated as aforementioned.

Yet, very few pheasants were to be found during the course of the shooting season. Allowing for the small number of birds and the extensive acreage involved, it was clear to me that the Black Hill was not holding these birds. The reason, which was pointed out to me by a local farmer, is that these birds almost always prefer to wander off *downhill*, and are reluctant to return to upland terrain. Consequently, wooded hills have to be made doubly attractive, and this means additional feeding, together with some hardwood, beech, or oak, in the forest. The warmth which firs offer for roosting is not sufficient. Therefore, it may well be to your advantage to plant a few of these yourself (with the landlord's permission, of course). I was fortunate in that the Forestry Commission decided to plant rows of oak trees for the purpose of future 'windbreaks' around the perimeter of my shoot. It was some five years, though, before the benefit of these were felt, and pheasants considered them worth foraging amongst.

ARTIFICIAL LANDSCAPES

We cannot overlook the fact that Forestry Commission woods are artificial, symmetrical rows of identical trees which make a mockery of the forests with which Nature has provided us for millions of years. It is also important that we fully understand the part which forestry plays in our national economy, for as shooting tenants of such woodlands we are under a moral obligation to safeguard their interests.

FORESTRY ROADS

It is doubtful whether the average person ever spares a thought to consider the usefulness of the thousands of miles of Forestry Commission roads throughout these islands of ours. They are taken for granted, and the only time when they are possibly appreciated is when the weekend visitor to the more remote parts of the countryside decides to take a walk in one of these vast artificial forests, and finds that he can do so with a minimum amount of effort and discomfort, and still have dry shoes at the end of it! Possibly these rough roads are mostly brought to the attention of the public during such events as the Monte Carlo Rally, and then are conveniently forgotten.

Let us first consider the purpose of this network of roadways throughout our national forests. They are not, as may fondly be imagined, constructed solely for the benefit of the hiker or the organisers of motor rallies. First and foremost they are a safeguard in the event of a forest fire, enabling the fire-engine to reach the blazing area as quickly and as easily as possible. In many places of afforestation, small reservoirs have been built at conveniently situated points, close to these roads, and thus a suply of water is usually not very far away from any possible source of fire.

The second use of these rough stone or slate roads is to speed up forestry work, providing easy access for vehicles, particularly in the case of felling. Timber can be carted away fairly easily and swiftly, whereas it would take twice as long if the Commission had to rely upon 'crawlers' to do this work over rough ground.

Forestry Commission roads are often constructed long after an area has been planted with trees, This may appear to the layman to be something of an afterthought, but in some cases it is purely a method of producing additional timber, using the land which the roads will occupy, to grow trees suitable for use as pit-props, and then, when these are matured, to fell them, combining the making of a road in the same process. The remaining timber will be left for some years then, and as the transportation of this will present much more of a problem when felled, then the roads will make that task so very much easier.

In many areas where fire-patrols are necessary at weekends and holiday times throughout the summer months, the forester-on-duty will be able to perform his work more efficiently, and with a great deal less physical exertion, if he is able to traverse the area under his charge in a

1-3 Forestry Roads—essential for fire control and transportation.

(photo: Guy Smith)

Plate 1

Top : Autumn in the Hills
Bottom : Pheasant on the Wing

motor vehicle. Trespassers and picnickers will be located before they have had a chance to do damage, in many cases, and the alarm can be raised that much quicker in the actual event of a fire being discovered.

DISADVANTAGES OF FORESTRY ROADS

However, there *are* drawbacks with these forestry roads, and in some areas they can be more than a disadvantage to the Commission than an advantage. Their main function, in providing ease of transport, can work both ways. Unless the main entrances are kept closed by means of locked gates, admission is simple to anybody at such times when vigilance is not being enforced. The learner-driver and the courting couple are probably the least harmful of all who may enter illegally. Others will drive vehicles in there under the cover of darkness, or sometimes brazenly in daylight, and help themselves liberally to young Christmas trees just prior to the Yuletide festival. Thieves will take advantage of easy access to steal on a large scale, and apart from lorry loads of trees, holly and ready-cut timber is there just for the taking.

The wild-life, too, will suffer a great deal of disturbance when these roads are first made in an area of hitherto perfect peace and quietness. The badger may find himself in the position of his human counterpart who finds a motorway scheduled to pass straight through his land. Whatever time of year the project is begun, it is almost certain to overlap into the breeding season for both birds and beasts. Except in the very smallest of woodlands, the work will not be completed in less than twelve months, probably taking very much longer if a hard winter is encountered when work is not possible at all for several weeks. One can usually expect an area in which the landscape is so structurally changed, to be almost devoid of wildlife until the job has been finished, and everything has had a chance to settle down again. Established rabbit-warrens will be swallowed up overnight, and the conies themselves will seek fresh pastures, far from the noise of bulldozers and mechanical saws. The hen pheasant will lay her eggs elsewhere, this particular season, as will any self-respecting wild-duck which happens to have found a convenient, usually quiet, woodland pool, within the proximity of these excavations.

It may take anything up to twelve months after the last stretch of road has been laid before any resemblance of normal woodland life returns. The rabbit, in many cases, finds the steep banks on either side

17

of the newly made roads ideal for burrowing in, and the hare enjoys basking in the sun here, its coat providing a natural camouflage on the sandy slopes. Likewise, the fox finds it a convenient place to lie in wait for both of these creatures, his natural prey, anyway. The sparrow-hawk glides along these new open spaces in the twilight and early dawn, whilst the more majestic buzzard soars above, hoping to surprise an unwary rabbit or perhaps a vole. All have accepted the change, and adapted themselves to it. We must do likewise, and not mis-use the privilege of being allowed to walk unhindered in these fast .increasing areas of woodland, checking on regulations beforehand with the local beat-forester. A copy of 'The Forestry Commission Byelaws' will gladly be supplied upon request, and in this phamplet are clearly stated the rules by which we must abide if we are to take advantage of the facilities available to us. Any shooting tenant would be well advised to carry a copy with him at all times so that he can clearly point out to miscreants the errors of their ways. It is strongly in his interests to prevent his shooting being abused, something which happens from time to time either through ignorance or deliberate vandalism by a small section of the general public. The majority are usually more than happy to co-operate, but it is from the minority that the danger stems.

Yet, a common fallacy exists that much of the land already discussed is "common land". This is not so, and it is the duty of every one of us, whether shooting tenant or weekend walker, to establish the law relating to this.

'COMMON LAND'

Nowadays "common land" is taken for granted by the general public. They fondly believe that the area in question belongs entirely to the people, and is there purely for their benefit, and for them to use it as they see fit. Campers, picnickers, tinkers, and week-end crowds from nearby urban areas treat it as their right, firmly believing that nobody has any authority to take them to task when they transgress.

In many cases these stretches of land belong to the local council, and it is the fact that they are often negligent in looking after it which creates this impression. Sometimes the respective council will lease it to a body such as the Forestry Commission or the National Coal Board. Stricter measures may be enforced in this case, the tenants interested in protecting their own welfare, but it is the untended and neglected acreages which suffer from the curse of irresponsible trespassers. I mention trespass, because except where there are defined rights-of-way, then the persons who walk there can quite legally be requested to leave.

There are many tracts of this latter type of common land throughout the country. Generally speaking, they are a disgrace. Apart from the usual litter which one would expect to find in these places, such as empty cigarette packets, sweet wrappers, and orange peel, one comes across abandoned cars, boxes of empty bottles (usually smashed!), and discarded furniture. No attempt is made to trace the culprits or to prevent further episodes. I did, however, hear of a case in one parish, where a family who were moving to the north of England, dumped a van load of rubbish on common land after dark on the eve of their departure. So confident were they that they had a right to do this, that they even included piles of old correspondence in amongst their unwanted items. As a result they were easily traced, and a prosecution followed.

Normally, common land is devoid of game, however attractive the woodlands may be to pheasants, or the open ground to partridges. This is largely due to the regular disturbance by trespassers, and their dogs which tear about wildly after a week of confinement within the limits of a town or city. Everywhere has a well-trodden look about it, and it is hard to imagine the landscape without a human being in sight. Only such birds as the jay and the magpie thrive here. They shriek and chatter from the thickets on a crowded bank holiday, knowing that the people there mean no harm, looking upon them as beautiful birds, perhaps related to the cockatoo or other such exotic species! They seem to know that their sworn enemy, the gamekeeper on the neighbouring estate, cannot molest them here.

I think that one of the best kept "common land" areas upon which I have ever set foot, is Kinver Edge in Staffordshire, owned by the National Trust. A resident warden is employed here, and although he has a large area to cover, he manages to enforce some degree of discilpline and authority on those who walk there. I have seen more pheasants here than on any other similar tract of land, and this alone speaks for itself. Admittedly, most of them have wandered there from adjoining preserves, but they would not do this if disturbance was rife.

One of the most barren commons which I have ever been on, if it can be placed in this category, is the Malvern Hills in Worcestershire. I have walked this land on many occasions, and beautiful as the scenery may be, there is, somehow, something missing. I realised, after only my first visit, that the lack of wildlife was conspicuous by its absence. Crows are the only form of birdlife which are in any way apparent. Once I saw a rabbit, but nothing else. I put this down to the fact that there are little or no woodlands there, a high altitude which is not conducive to game and wildlife in general, and from April to September, every year, never free of ramblers and picnickers.

FIRE DANGER

A tightening up on restrictions which can legally be enforced over "common land" would be of benefit to the whole country. Fire is the main danger to all such land, and during fine week-ends in the summer, somewhere there will always be a blaze which requires the attention of the fire brigade before it is finally extinguished. There are many causes for these fires. Perhaps a broken bottle in the rays of the midday sun will ignite some dry heather or bracken. On the other hand, a group of youths, bent on mischief and totally ignorant of the ways of the countryside, may deliberately apply a lighted match to the undergrowth. The damage may be negligible in one place, whilst in another thousands of pounds of growing timber may be destroyed. Likewise, the nearest fire brigades will be called out at a time when their presence elsewhere is more urgently needed.

The public, when orderly and well behaved, are an asset to any common. Their presence there during the summer months can be invaluable. A fire may thus be prevented in its early stages, or else the fire brigade summoned in time to prevent it gaining a hold and spreading. I am of the opinion that it would be beneficial to all councils owning this type of land to encourage the public to visit it, but also to attempt to confine them to a specific area, allowing the woodlands to remain undisturbed, and wildlife to remain there, and, perhaps, to breed. One way of achieving this object would be to place benches and rustic garden furniture in ideally situated places. Many picnickers would be tempted to use these rather than to venture further afield. This amenity would be appreciated, I have no doubt, both by the people who take advantage of them, and also by the hen pheasant which is attempting to hatch a clutch of eggs in some rough cover only a short distance away.

These Forestry Commission byelaws incorporate many ways of eliminating hooliganism and co-operating with the public at the same time. Various councils throughout the British Isles could do far worse than follow their example. Perhaps then, the term "common land" would have a different meaning to those who wander there during their leasure hours, and instil a degree of responsibility into them.

Never before has our wildlife been so dependent upon mankind for survival. Conservation and sport must walk hand-in-hand. There is no dividing line.

BEING PREPARED

Being properly clothed and equipped is a vital requirement for upland shooting: the essentials are as follows:

CLOTHING

There are no hard and fast rules regarding the type of clothing necessary for hill-shooting. In such areas the weather is likely to change without warning, but whereas the wildfowler wears heavy garments to keep him warm and dry throughout a long vigil on the marshes, the hill-shooter is constantly on the move over rugged terrain. Only during pigeon-shooting or duck-flighting is he likely to suffer from the cold. He will, though, have to brave torrential rain and blinding snowstorms.

During the winter months it is better to wear light under garments and rely upon weatherproof top clothing to combat the elements. Some thought should be given to the latter, There are many excellent waterproof coats on the market today, but some of them are apt to restrict movement and to hamper the sportsman when a snap-shot is necessary. A zipper-coat is possibly best for keeping dry in heavy rain, and can be worn unfastened for the rest of the time, allowing the air to circulate beneath it.

Waterproof trousers are cumbersome, and unless of the thornproof variety they are likely to tear easily on briars. A *light* pair of thigh-length waders, turned down during dry weather, are probably more comfortable, and when that threatening storm finally breaks they can be pulled up instantly. Some form of headgear is essential in any form of shooting, for nothing shows up more plainly to the oncoming bird than the human face. Yet, on the hills, a hat is even more vital. Soaking wet hair can lead to a cold, influenza, or even pneumonia. You will be out in the wilds for hours on end so you may as well be comfortable and enjoy your sport.

Your hat should blend with your surroundings. There are many camouflaged and reasonably-priced ones available today which are also waterproof. Many of these would not meet with the approval of a conventional gameshooter, but up in the hills they are ideal. Here, and on the saltings, are two places where etiquette of dress matters not.

A wide brim will prevent the rain from dripping down your neck. Some prefer the deerstalker style with ear-muffs to use if caught in a sudden snowstorm. It is all a matter of individual choice.

However elaborate your weatherproof clothing, it is always advisable to carry a few dry garments in your car. Most of us who follow this type of sport have a long journey home afterwards, and an hour of discomfort at this stage can turn an otherwise enjoyable day into an unpleasant memory.

GUNS

As with every branch of the sport of shooting there is a particular gun which suits each individual. There are no rules laid down. We have the experienced wildfowler who claims to kill all his geese with a standard 2½in. chambered 12-bore, and no doubt would find himself at a disadvantage with a heavy magnum. Yet he is an exception to the rule. Most fowlers carry heavier weapons, 2¾ or 3in. chambered magnums. So it is with hill-shooting.

Experimenting is a costly business nowadays, and it is preferable to settle for a gun which will give you good service right from the start. In order to help you with your choice it is advisable to look at the land over which you will shoot. You need a gun which you can carry comfortably over steep ground, and still be able to shoot with it towards the close of the day. Seldom, though, will your shots be easy or close. In a way you are an 'inland-upland wildfowler', but a magnum gun will weigh too heavy for you and a light one will be at a disadvantage where long shots are the order of the day.

The average gun most suitable for hill shooting is the 12-bore with 2¾in. chambers, with barrels no longer than 28 inches, the left full-choke, the right half-choke. You have here a weapon which is light enough to carry, yet capable of dealing with almost any type of quarry at ranges up to 40 yards.

An expensive gun is not necessary. It will have some rough wear during the course of a normal day's shooting, but cleaned regularly and maintained by a reliable gunsmith it should give you years of service.

CARTRIDGES

As with the gun, the cartridge is a personal choice. It must, out of necessity, under these conditions be a hard-hitting one. For many years the author has loaded his own ammunition, but in recent months has taken to using an American brand with the comparatively recent innovation of a Plaswad. This wad is cup-shaped, in some ways resembling a badminton shuttlecock, and holds the shot together longer, thereby increasing the density of the pattern. The only shot-size available was 7½, designed for clay-pigeon shooting, but they have proved more than suitable for rabbit, hare, duck, and pigeon. This, surely, is proof enough that pattern is more important than penetration.

Nevertheless, for the beginner with a standard gun, 5 or 6 shot is quite adequate. Modern plastic cases have eliminated the damp and swollen ammunition which we used to experience regularly a few years ago. In fact, never before have we had such a choice of guns and ammunition at our disposal. In many ways it is all rather bewildering for the beginner, and it is hoped that the advice given here will save him both time and money.

HILL SHOOTING AND UPLAND GAMEKEEPING

CHAPTER 2

Corvines and Birds of Prey

Even in this enlightened age when people are taking more and more interest in the wildlife which abounds in our rapidly diminishing tracts of countryside, the ignorance of a small minority never ceases to amaze me, or sometimes even to amuse me when incorrect 'sightings' are made by those who purport to know their natural history.

MISINTERPRETATIONS OF WILDLIFE

Some years ago I bought a guide-book describing the area surrounding my 600 acres of hill-shooting in south Shropshire. I purchased it purely out of interest, whilst in the village newsagent's shop, for the modest sum of 17½p.

I certainly had my money's worth out of that little booklet, affording myself as much pleasure from its inexactitudes as I did from its wealth of valuable information. Having read it, and digested it (page 37 was printed upside down!) I could not help but reflect on the section covering the wildlife in the area.

The author stated that my own shoot is visited by 'ospreys and peregrine-falcons'. Curlew are in abundance, as are grouse and blackcock! I was rendered incapable of comment for some minutes after reading this, wondering in my own mind if I had explored my own area fully, or whether he had made a gigantic geographical error. However, neither was the case, and all I can conclude is that the writer's ornithology did not compare with his archaeology, and knowledge of local folklore.

Whilst not wishing to condemn this worthy man's observations on bird life in general, I analysed each species he had mentioned, and then made a note of one or two which he had omitted. Regarding ospreys, I cannot, in my wildest imagination, visualize one of these sea-hawks gliding over my forestry plantations. The small woodland pool in the centre does not even contain fish, so this noble bird would certainly have a lean time of it up there.

Where did this ghastly error spring from? Perhaps it originated way back in 1964, on one warm April day. It was then, in the company of a knowledgeable friend who supported my observations, that I saw a kite. A bird of passage, admittedly, but it had visited my shoot nevertheless. Further enquiries revealed that the tall trees, so greatly favoured by these majestic birds in the "Valley of the Kites" in Wales, had been felled. The kites had dispersed, and no doubt it was one of these, seeking new territoties, which I had seen. Was this the osprey of the guide-book? I strongly suspect that it may well have been, the writer being misinformed by a casual observer who had jumped to a hasty conclusion.

I heartily wish that I had the abundance of grouse and blackgame which I am *reputed* to have on my land. I believe there are still grouse in the Shropshire hills, although I have never seen any, but I doubt whether the larger species is to be seen there today. I once had a sight of an ancient game register, before the Forestry Commission destroyed the acres of heather by planting young fir trees, just after the second world war. Both grouse and blackgame featured prominently.

I spoke with the elderly farmer who shot the last grouse in the area, way back in 1941. He recalled how their call could be heard regularly, morning and evening, on the hills behind his house. Gradually they became heard less and less, until finally they disappeared entirely from the rural scene. I will not blame the Forestry Commission altogether for this loss, for the decline really started during the war years when the gamekeepers were focusing their sights on targets of a more serious nature. 'Muir burning' was neglected, the heather grew old and coarse, lacking the fresh young shoots so vital to the existence of grouse and blackgame, and they were forced to seek fresh pastures, or die of starvation.

The writer mentions the presence of curlew, again localising them on my own particular ground. He leaves the reader with the impression that these long-beaked birds, with the lonely, warbling cry, can be seen there at any time. This is not the case, however, for they arrive in the early spring, and depart again in late summer. The hills and moorlands are merely a breeding ground for curlew, their natural habitat being mainly costal regions, and sometimes inland lakes and marshes.

The writer of this otherwise excellent little booklet, quite correctly mentions Ravens as being fairly common in these beautiful hills. However, he completely ignores the buzzard, a much more interesting and graceful bird. Buzzards are now on the increase after years of fighting for survival, a state of affairs bought about largely by a shortage of rabbits, their natural food, with the outbreak of myxomatosis. However, as the rabbits began increasing so did these large, stately hawks. Only last summer, whilst engaged on some keepering duties, I came upon a most amazing scene in a grass field bordering my woodlands. A sheep had died, unknown to the farmer, possibly a few days beforehand, and circling above, some already settled upon it, I counted seventeen ravens and nine buzzards. The majority of the former were busy mobbing the latter, whilst a few of their more cunning and farseeing brethren were feasting on the object of their presence there. There was no question, certainly, of either species being even remotely in danger of extinction in the light of this evidence.

I have seen an abundance of sparrowhawks lately in this area, but the number of woodpigeon remains, which I have come across, tells of many more of which I have not caught sight of. This is encouraging, for only in recent years these birds also were on the decline.

This guide-book contains many historical and legendary accounts of great interest to the visitor to this part of the Shropshire/Welsh borderland, and the labour involved in compiling the whole work, would, no doubt, have taken up months of the author's time in research, and travelling to the various places. However, too many local publications, such as these, tend to disregard or misinterpret the subject of wildlife. It is a great pity, especially in the case of such readers as myself who usually turn to this section of the book first. It could also serve to send hosts of misinformed amateur ornithologists on a search for mythical ospreys or peregrine-falcons. Perhaps one of these birds did happen in the area at some time in the past, a lost bird blown off course by a strong gale, but it will be years before one is seen there again, if at all. Our countryside today is more precious than ever, and we must guard it to the best of our ability. Only in this way will we be able to preserve it for the next generation, and educate them accordingly.

RAVENS

The Raven, however, is commonplace. This large corvine, possibly half as big again as its cousin, the carrion crow, is to be heard frequently 'cronking' across the hills and valleys, his deep call so distinctive. If one pauses for a while, and watches, before long one will see this bird flapping over the dense spruce thickets, his sharp eyes searching diligently for any carrion which will provide him with food. Sometimes, he will soar and glide at a great hight, in a similar fashion to the buzzard.

The raven, of course, is protected by law, but the all important question is whether or not he is detrimental to game. Most definitely he is an egg-hunter, for I have seen one flying off with an egg which a careless 'free-range' hen had laid some distance from the orchard, where one of my farmer-friends keeps his poultry. This bird has exactly the same tendencies as his other corvine cousins, the only consolation being that Ravens are much less numerous than crows, at the moment, anyway.

I firmly believe, however, that the Raven confines most of his hunting to the sheep fields. I cannot excuse his attacks on helpless, newborn lambs, and ewes which find themselves in trouble whilst giving birth, but, on the whole, he is content to feed upon the odd dead carcase. Perhaps it is fortunate, therefore, that hill-farmers, in desolate areas, are somewhat dilatory regarding the burial of dead sheep.

However, rogue and scavenger that he may be, the Raven is, nevertheless, a most interesting bird. I well remember the day when a friend of mine scaled a 50 ft. Scots pine, in order to investigate the nest of one of these birds. From where I stood on the ground below, I could see that this massive structure, built in the topmost boughs, had a circumference of about 6 ft. However, it was my colleague who provided the 'inside story'. The nest itself must have been in use for many years, for new layers were easily discernible where the birds had renovated and extended their home each successive spring. Only twigs and moss were used, and no mud or soil had been taken up there to line it. So sound was it, that even the wind could not penetrate its interior, and the thick fir branches above acted as a roof. It was, indeed, a very snug home, and it was a great pity when a new farmer felled this delightful spinney in order to increasing his grazing land. I had already named it 'Raven Wood'.

The Raven's chief enemy, in these parts, anyway, is the buzzard, although the corvine is usually the more aggressive when it comes to open conflict. I once witnessed a battle between these two species, during the nesting season. A buzzard had ventured too close to the Ravens' nest, and it was the cock Raven who dived into the attack from above, whilst the hen bird was busy sitting on her eggs. It was certainly a royal conflict, although most of the action was confined to diving and feinting, with a fair amount of insults being flung by both contestants at their respective foe. In the end, it was the buzzard who conceded defeat, graceful even in retreat.

Ravens, along with buzzards, have increased greatly during the last ten years or so. It was their decline which was responsible for them becoming a protected bird, but, should they multiply at the same rate as the rook and carrion crow, then they would have to be removed from legal safety. Tradition has much to do with the favourable light in which they are viewed by the general public, and, no doubt, it is their royal relations in the Tower of London which have been responsible for the leniency shown towards them. Superstition has it that if ever the Ravens should desert the Tower, then England would fall to a foreign foe. Thus, someone surmised, a population of these birds must be maintained in the country, at all costs. It would, indeed, be a sad day if the Raven approached extinction, but, from the numbers I see regularly, I cannot foresee that happening. However, some form of control could be necessary before long. It will be difficult, indeed, to ensure that the right balance is maintained, It will be a question of striking a happy medium, but first I think that a nationwide effort chould be made to reduce the country's crow and rook population. Gamekeepers who are working conscientiously towards this end, are constantly thwarted by large tracts of unkeepered land where all members of the corvine tribe are allowed to breed at will. If this obstacle could be overcome, then I do not think anybody, whether they be gamekeepers or ornithologists, would object to a reasonable increase of Ravens.

In addition to my rented acreage of shooting rights, consisting of one of the hills in that range on the borders of Shropshire and Radnorshire, my lease also covers an adjoining valley. This latter is, in some respects, similar to the former, and in others totally in contrast.

A narrow country road, not wide enough for two cars to pass without one or the other of them pulling on to the grass verge, separates my two pieces of land. A wire-netting fence runs along the top of this valley, principally erected in the hope of preventing rabbits from entering and damaging the spruce trees, but its main function nowadays is to safeguard the unwary week-end motorist from venturing too close to the precipitous slopes.

For the first year or so of my tenancy I regarded this valley (locally known as 'the Dingle', because of the narrow mountain stream which wends its way along the bottom) as a waste of time and energy, the long climb down, and the return journey being equally undesirable, not purely on account of the physical exertion required, but because of the masses of gorse bushes which had rapidly sprung up, and spread along the lines of artificially planted trees. Seldom did one escape without a trouser seat full of prickles, and usually scratched hands as well when attempting to break the fall.

It was after the felling of the "Raven Wood", that privately owned length of woodland adjoining the upper slopes of my 'Dingle' that I began to concentrate more on the lower regions of my land. Until then I had had far too many interesting places on the higher land with which to occupy myself. However, with the destruction of that nest which had been the home of a pair of these large corvines for some years, I felt as a gardener might feel who has had half his garden taken from him in a road-widening scheme.

Thus, I began to spend more and more time in my little valley. The forested slope on the side adjoining the road was virtually useless as far as the sporting potential was concerned. The gorse and bracken grew denser each year, and the few rabbits which had found their way there could move unseen beneath this undergrowth. The far side was privately owned by the farmer whose fields ran parallel, and although I had no right to cross the stream, this part was of great interest to me. There were about three acres of very ancient, gigantic larch trees. Misshapen, twisted and gnarled by the westerly winds which howled through the length of the valley, they served to remind the visitor of the days when forestry was conducted on a far less scientific and economic basis. Trees were just planted, not in the uninteresting straight rows of modern afforestation, but in a haphazard fashion with no thought given to intensive timber production. It was a well spaced wood, with virtually no undergrowth apart from a carpet of thick spiky grass and the odd bramble bush. Adjoining it was a further couple of acres of thickly planted hawthorn bushes, the purpose of which I am unable to determine, unless it was intended as shelter for sheep and cattle during hard weather, in which case I would have thought a belt of spruce would have been considerably more comfortable as far as the poor beasts were concerned.

I discovered that this valley was considerably more interesting from a wild-life point of view than the adjoining hills. It is certainly a degree or two warmer down here in winter, and consequently the woodpigeons find it more acceptable. The buzzards and sparrow-hawks come here after the pigeons, and usually there are several crows bent on mobbing these birds of prey. There is plenty of activity for the keen ornithologist, and always the chance of a shot for the keen sportsman. The bracken covered banks of the stream usually hold either a rabbit or a hare, and occasionally a cock pheasant will come clattering out at the approach of a dog, either to fall with a splash into the rushing water below, or else to gain the safety of the upper regions with a defiant 'cock-up' as he disappears over the brow of the hill.

It was just twelve months after the destruction of 'Raven Wood' that I heard one of the most thrilling sounds which I think I have ever heard in the countryside. I had long since resigned myself to the absence of that particular pair of birds which had been in the vicinity for so long. Admittedly ravens passed over from time to time, but none were *resident.* I had none to call my own.

Then, in mid-April, whilst looking for signs of an increase in my rabbit population alongside the Dingle, I heard, unmistakably, the 'cronk' of a raven from the larch wood opposite. It was not the deep throated call of the adult corvine, but the more crowlike one of the fledgling. Leaving my gun on my own side of the fence, I waded the stream, and climbed up into my neighbour's wood.

At first I could see nothing, and then a large black shape glided over the treetops above me, harshly chiding me in a voice I knew so well. The female bird was not irate without reason, and full of hope I pressed on.

In the very centre of this weather-beaten spinney, I saw that which I had hardly hoped to see. Constructed in the fork of two massive branches, and supported by the trunk, only a couple of feet or so from the very top of the massive larch tree, was a brand new raven's nest. However, my attention was only focused on this for a few seconds, for

31

there, barely a yard from it, perched two young birds, already the size of carrion crows. They had not yet attained their full powers of flight, and were still 'flappers', jostling from branch to branch, relying on their parents to provide them with food.

My step was brisk and my heart was light as I made my way back to the 'Dingle', and waded across, back to my own land. The ravens had returned, and I knew now that they would stay. Their determination to remain in the vicinity had triumphed even in the face of modern agricultural methods.

SPARROW-HAWKS

It seemed, only a short time ago, that many of our native hawks were bordering on extinction. Of course, this state of affairs began with the outbreak of myxomatosis back in the early fifties. The buzzard, particularly, was deprived of its staple diet, and its numbers dwindled alarmingly. A vicious circle had begun.

Most recent of all, though, the sparrowhawk has been battling for survival, and only now has it shown any signs of a comeback. It was the last of the species to be afforded protection by law.

Early last summer I witnessed a sparrowhawk taking a woodpigeon on the wing. The latter was totally unaware of its presence until its enemy suddenly appeared above it. Escape was out of the question, and the luckless pigeon plummetted earthwards in a cloud of feathers. A couple of hundred yards further on I disturbed the hawk at its meal. Purely out of curiosity, I examined the kill. The breast was ripped open where this hunter of the skies had already begun to feed, but it was the pigeon's head which interested me most. A deep gash showed where one of the wicked talons had struck it *in flight!*

Yet, the sparrowhawk for too long has been persecuted by game-preservers. The fact that this bird helps itself to the odd pheasant or partridge chick is no excuse for the ruthlessness with which it was once pursued by gamekeepers. Fortunately, today, these men are more enlightened, and recognise the sparrowhawk as being part of Nature's plans to effect a balance throughout all wildlife.

The kestrel is probably the most prolific of all hawks today. It is the gentlest of the species, surviving mostly on mice, voles, and young rats. It is easily identified by its hovering technique. It will remain almost motionless in mid-air, except for a slight movement of wings, as it hovers, watching and waiting. Perhaps it has spotted a mouse darting into a tussock of grass, and is hoping that it will emerge again.

This bird, too, has been wrongly listed as an enemy of game. Occasionally, a 'rogue' kestrel will help itself to a chick from the gamekeeper's rearing-field. Yet, this is an exception. The kestrel is usually quite content to feed on small rodents.

Birds of prey are part of our heritage. Their protection is of paramount importance. The good which they do in the countryside far outweighs their transgressions. They do much to control the rodent population, assisted, of course, by the various species of owls which may also be classed as birds of prey. Neither game-birds nor songsters have ever really suffered by their presence. Yet, the misdeeds of the odd hawk, years ago, brought the species into disrepute with gamekeepers who declared that "if it's got a hooked beak—kill it!"

Perhaps, with intensive conservation, we shall be able to rectify much of the damage perpetrated by the last generation. The withdrawal of every one of the hawks from the gamekeeper's 'vermin list' is probably the greatest step in this direction. We hope that we are not too late, and that, in years to come, these hawks, which were once a common sight, may yet again grace our countryside with their presence.

BUZZARD WOOD

I have alrady related how 'Raven Wood' was deliberately destroyed in the interests of agriculture. A matter of a few years later a similar disaster was destined to destroy a wood which for decades had been the home of that most stately of all hawks, the buzzard. Ironically, though, this time it was Nature herself who brought about the desecration. In no way could the tragedy be attributed to mankind's ceaseless quest for progress and the relentless march of civilization.

On the steep slopes of a Welsh border mountainside, divided by a narrow road that turns back on itself in a sharp hairpin bend, stands the remains of twenty acres of giant Scots pines. For decades, as long as the inhabitants of the small village below can remember, this has been the home of buzzards, those slow flying, yet magnificently graceful predators of the air. With ragged wings scarcely moving, the occupants of Buzzard Wood have hunted the hillsides and grazing fields in search of small prey and carrion. Often their fare has been sparse, particularly during those years when myxomatosis was at its height, yet somehow they survived.

33

This wood was never devoid of buzzards, and in the last few years the shepherds and hill-farmers have watched these birds increase. One spring three separate nests produced young, and the mewing of these large hawks was an accompaniment to the constant bleating of sheep on the slopes above Buzzard Wood.

One day, of course, these trees would most certainly be felled, having long since passed their prime, but perhaps their owner, a true lover of the countryside, was postponing that day until it was absolutely necessary, realising that he would be destroying the stronghold of generations of buzzards. This was the opinion of villagers and farmers alike.

Then, on the night of January 2nd, 1976, Nature herself decreed that these giant 50 year-old trees must come down. The westerly winds, which had been freshening throughout the day, increased to unbelievable force with the coming of dusk. Pines which had the strength of stone pillars, bent before the gusts, creaking and groaning as their massive roots took the strain. For two or three hours they defied the elements, but as the hurricane finally reached full force, they yielded to a might greater than their own. Then, in their darkest hour, they began to fall. The villagers, shelting from the blast in their snug whitewashed cottages, heard the crashes of falling trees, but it was daylight before they were to become aware of the true extent of the damage which the whirlwind had left in its wake.

Remarkably, the village itself suffered little. Buzzard Wood had taken the full force of the gale, destroying itself in its protection of mankind. It took two whole days before the roads were cleared sufficiently for anybody to be able to reach the wood in order to survey the full extent of the damage. The 'Castle Tree', a mighty pine that had supported a buzzard's nest, occupied by breeding birds for years, lay on the ground, two lesser trees splintered beneath it. Some trees still remained standing, these being comparatively younger ones, the roots of which had been able to hold the lighter weight, and also had somehow miraculously escaped the falling giants.

Of the buzzards there was no sign. Several old nests were examined, their structures reinforced with growing moss, and solidified droppings. No doubt their instinct had warned the hawks to roost elsewhere on that fateful night, probably deep in the artificial Forestry Commission woods, a mile or so away, where even these terrible gales had not been able to disturb their nocturnal rest.

It was with a feeling of sadness that I watched the clearing-up operations a few days later. Heavy machinery and power-driven saws rapidly removed the debris, and timber that should have been transported to the saw-mills years ago was finally sent on its belated journey.

All that remained was a mere skeleton of the old Buzzard Wood which so many in that small community had known for so long. As I stood and looked at the open spaces where once majestic trees towered up into the sky above, movement attracted my attention. As I looked up, I saw a buzzard soaring above me, its moth-like wings stationary in the still atmosphere. Perhaps it was hunting its daily prey, or had it returned to view the ruins of its former home? I watched as it glided further away, hunting the sheep-fields, yet it also seemed to have a destination in mind—those Forestry Commission thickets. There was no doubt in my mind that this was where the inhabitants of Buzzard Wood had gone. Perhaps it would only be a temporary residence during the intervening span of time whilst those trees which had escaped the hurricane matured, or would the buzzards settle for their new home?

That is something which only time will reveal, and it will probably be several years before we know whether the buzzards of Buzzard Wood have left for good, or if it is their intention to return to that tract of woodland which was once their domain, the sanctuary in which they roosted and bred, reared their young, and new generations succeeded the aged and ailing. Nature has destroyed, and it is She who will rebuild.

THE ROOK-SHOOTS OF YESTERYEAR

The old Rookery still stands beyond the big house. They are the same trees that were there fifty years ago, the spreading branches providing a roof overhead when the foliage is in full growth, screening the sunlight, and making the interior dark and gloomy. The ferny floor was white with droppings of the raucous black birds which breed here every spring, and somehow the visitor finds himself moving stealthily as if in awe of some majestic place of worship.

When I visited the Rookery last spring memories came flooding back to me of days long gone, the annual rook-shoots and the accompanying house parties. Nothing so grand takes place today. Indeed, this rookery has not had a shot fired in it for thirty years. The number of nests has increased, and the remnant wild birds of a once plentiful stock of game need to camouflage their clutches well in order to escape the sharp eyes of these corvine predators.

Old Sam the keeper has gone, too, and has never been replaced. Here and there are the rotting remnants of a release-pen, the bracken and briars growing through the rusted wiremesh. Sam loved his charges with a deep devotion, and I was told of his expression of delight one November when more birds than usual had crossed the line of guns outside the Home Covert. His own job had been executed with efficiency, and he was not responsible for the poor markmanship of the squire's guests. The size of the bag worried him least of all.

Yet, rook shooting was in complete contrast to those autumnal pheasant drives. Another cycle had begun in the gamekeeper's year, the leaf was fresh and green again, and the control of these rooks had an important bearing on the success of the rearing season which lay ahead.

There was nothing casual about these rook shoots, though. May 12th was a date of equal importance to August 12th as far as the squire was concerned. Full shooting dress was expected of all the guests, and woe betide he who turned up in flannels and shirt sleeves. Nobody was allowed to load until the Rookery was surrounded, and the Squire personally blew a whistle to inform all and sundry that shooting may begin.

Sam and two keepers from the adjoining estate went into the wood itself with their rook-rifles, weapons which seemed only to have an annual outing. Twenty or so guns surrounded the Rookery, waiting with all the apprehension of a partridge drive, listening to the almost deafening cawing of the quarry, and then the quarrelsome notes changing to anger and surprise as the rifles barked their first messages of death.

One particular year the birds had nested early. The young were already more advanced than just the 'branching' stage, but the Squire would not hear of shooting early. May 12th was . . . well, May 12th!

A black cloud rose above the treetops, young rooks testing the full power of their untried wings, many dropping back as the effort proved too much for them. The adult birds were the first to leave, a dozen or so of them falling at once to the barrage of shotgun fire, the survivors fighting to gain height, then circling and hurling angry insults at the shooters below.

36

The gunfire increased as more and more birds-of-the-year attempted to cross the open fields to the safety of the Home Covert. The few which did manage to reach the tall oaks found sanctuary, for the Squire would allow no shooting inside the main pheasant wood, under any circumstances, until October 1st. Even Sam was forced to confine his constant war on vermin to traps and snares within that haven during the close season.

A lull in the shooting followed. The marksmen inside the Rookery moved quietly from tree to tree, their position only being revealed to those outside by the occasional crack of a rifle and the whine of a slug. The area was too great for three of them to cover it adequately, but the Squire was adamant about no more than three riflemen being allowed to pick off the branchers. Eventually, they disturbed a fresh colony of birds, and another battue opened up as the shotguns went into action against the 'fliers'.

Dusk fell at last, much later than our May twilight today for it was wartime, and everyone was blessed, or cursed, with additional daylight. Rooks cawed their disapproval from the Home Covert, and those remaining in the Rookery answerd them. Sam's two teenage sons concluded the last of the picking-up, dragging heavy sacks in their wake, and uttering loud exclamations every time they came across another dead bird.

Then it was back to the Hall, and a lavish buffet. Whole hams, pickles, salad vegetables from the extensive kitchen gardens, followed by fresh strawberries and cream. Throughout all this there was no sign of Sam, his gamekeeper colleagues, or their sons. They were busy with the count, laying out the rooks in long rows on the floor of the barn, then tying them into bunches of six for the guests to take away with them. 496 was the final total, and perhaps it was the fault of the pickers-up that the party had not made the 500!

Then it was back to the reality of a war that was almost over, and the promise of better times. Yet, much was left behind, occasions such as the 'glorious lesser 12th'. These functions were to remain but pleasant memories during those dark days of war, and the rook itself suffered a fall in status when our countryside was hard hit by the breaking up of many of the larger estates. We had sacrificed more than we thought in the cause of freedom. Even in times of extortionate food prices, rookpie is considered to be too humble a fare.

I have a secret ambition to revive those old rook-shooting parties. Perhaps one day, if I can persuade the new owner of the Hall, these border hills will once again echo concentrated gunfire on May 12th!

KILLING GAME

It is essential that the shooter is fully conversant with the species which he may kill, those that are afforded 'close' seasons (i.e. when shooting is not allowed), those for which a game-licence is required, and also those which are afforded full protection by law. It is for this purpose that the following tables are given:

GAME

A game-licence must be held before any of these can be taken:

Species	Close-Season
Pheasant	February 2nd-September 30th
Partridge	February 2nd-August 31st
Grouse	December 11th-August 11th
Ptarmigan	December 11th-August 11th
Black Game	December 11th-August 19th
Hare	No close season, but may not be offered *for sale* between March 1st and July 31st
Snipe	February 1st-August 11th
Woodcock—*England and Wales*	February 1st-September 30th
Scotland	February 1st-August 31st

Note: It is illegal to take game on Sundays or on Christmas Day. In some counties, and in Scotland, Sunday shooting is forbidden, and if in doubt check with local authorities.

Species which may be taken at any time subject to regulations forbidding shooting on Sundays and Christmas Day. No game licence is necessary:—

Woodpigeon, Rabbit, Rook, Carrion Crow, Jackdaw, Magpie, Jay, Grey Squirrel, Stoat, Weasel, Polecat, Rat, Fox.

Wild duck and geese may be shot in areas *above* high-water mark between September 1st and January 31st. In coastal areas *below* high-water mark this period is extended to February 20th, as the majority of birds shot here are migratory species and are unlikely to be pairing up prior to nesting before this date.

PROTECTED SPECIES WHICH MAY *NOT* BE KILLED AT ANY TIME

It is thought only necessary to list here those that are likely to be encountered by the hillshooter; they may *not* be killed and are as follows:

Hawks—all species

Raven

Lapwing

Green Woodpecker

It is also important that the beginners learn to differentiate between woodpigeons and racing-pigeons. The latter are likely to be encountered almost anywhere at any time. Apart from the difference in colouring, the mode of flight is probably the best guide. The bird which flies on a straight course, and does not swerve and alter direction when it sees you out in the open, is almost sure to be a racer.

The penalties for shooting racingpigeons, protected birds, and species during their close-seasons are heavy, and could bring about the confiscation of your gun. Don't chance it. **If you are not certain of identification, then hold your fire!**

39

CHAPTER 3

Which Species are Vermin?
An Army of Rats on the move

CLASSIFICATION OF VERMIN

One man's meat is another man's poison. A very old, but true, saying indeed, and how aptly it can be applied to the controversial question of which species of wildlife are to come under the heading of 'vermin', in our present-day countryside.

The **rat** is probably the only creature which is regarded as vermin in all walks of life, whether urban or rural. I have yet to hear a good word spoken of this rodent, for his depredations are known to all, and there is always the chance that he may carry disease with him as he scavenges.

The **hedgehog** is a true Jekyll and Hyde. From the gardener's point of view he is an invaluable ally as he moves amongst the vegetable patch, after dark, feeding on grubs and slugs which are detrimental to growing crops. However, once he crosses the boundary on to the nearby estate, he is no longer interested in these small pests, for a meal of pheasant or partridge egge is much tastier, and far more nourishing. He will, therefore, find the gamekeeper a very different prospect from the friendly gardener. Instead of a saucer of bread and milk, placed conveniently for him to find at nightfall, he is likely to step into a well-sited tunnel trap, or meet with a charge of shot. It is a great pity that our prickly friend is unable to appreciate the sanctuary of a spacious garden, for he would then be able to live in peace, and be looked upon as a friend rather than a foe.

In the fruit-growing areas of this country, the **bullfinch** tops the "wanted" list. He cannot resist the buds of fruit trees during April and May, and, in certain areas, there are special dispensations allowing these birds to be shot. Elsewhere they are on the protected list, and he who is foolish enough to kill one of these colourful pillagers of orchards can expect to be punished severely. One can appreciate the fruit-farmer's

41

3-1 A Stoat—a real enemy.   (Drawing by Bob Sanders)

point of view, and also sympathise with the orchard-owner who is restricted in the way in which he protects his crops. To the householder, whose garden is without apple trees, the bullfinch is an interesting, and welcome visitor. What a pity it is that these birds cannot change their diet!

The **rook**, too, enjoys both popularity and unpopularity. Next to the rat, this corvine is probably the worst enemy of the gamepreserver. His hunt for eggs of gamebirds during the spring is relentless. He has the sharpest of eyesight, and a nest has to be well hidden in dense undergrowth in order to be free of his unwelcome attentions. However, the non-shooting farmer looks upon him in an entirely different light. A flock of rooks will follow the plough for days on end, eagerly devouring any wire-worms which are unearthed. One cannot deny that they are doing a useful job of work in ridding the land of these pests, but my answer to this argument is that there are enough plover and seagulls only too happy to carry out this work for them. The faults of these latter two species in no way compares with those of the rook. The **gull** may rob the odd nest if he happens to spot one sited in an open space, but seldom will he search for one. The **plover** is one of the most harmless of birds.

The week-end visitor to the countryside is enthralled by the beautiful colourings of the **jay** as this rascally bird flits through the thickets shouting his harsh warning of the presence of man to all and sundry. However, if only these urban dwellers were to witness the remnants of a nest, perhaps that of a blackbird or thrush, which the jay has plundered, then I am sure that the praise bestowed upon the villain would be considerably lessened.

The game-preserver is probably in the best position to judge the merits and faults of those species of wildlife which so loosely come under the heading of "vermin". One must approach the subject with an open mind, for the aim is to control those predators which can be lawfully killed, and not to exterminate them. The target is to maintain a balance of nature, and by doing this we shall all benefit, whether we are gardeners, fruit-farmers, or conservationists.

ARMIES OF RATS ON THE MOVE

I wonder how many people remember the invasion of Shropshire by "vast armies of rats", as the press reported it, some years ago. The border counties, according to the various accounts, were the ones which

3-2 A grey Squirrel: attractive but destructive

(Anthea Hadley from a drawing by Bob Sanders)

suffered most. Granaries were raided, growing crops were ravaged, and countryside dwellers lived in fear of the grey scourge descending on them overnight.

During this time I increased my number of tunnel-traps on my shoot in the hills above Clun. I fully expected my 'hoppers', containing barley, to be plundered, and my woodlands to be overrun with these rodents. *But nothing happened.* It seemed to me that the whole affair was a non-event, a rumour started by some farmer who had perhaps unearthed an unusually large colony of rats in one of his cornstacks, or in the demolition of some old farm-buildings.

This was my own opinion, and I stood firmly by it, until one night I was faced with a scene which caused me completely to change my views on the subject. It was about a week prior to Christmas, and the whole countryside was covered by a light fall of snow. There was a full moon, and a sharp frost caused the snow to sparkle crisply, every landmark being as visible as it would have been in broad daylight.

On this particular night I had lingered over a pint of ale in one of the excellent inns in Clun, after a hard day's shooting over my steep terrain, and consequently it was much later than usual when I eventually drove homewards in the direction of Craven Arms. On my right the River Clun was plainly visible, twisting its way like a black serpent through a white landscape. Suddenly, out of the corner of my eye, I noticed a movement, somewhere along the nearside bank. It could have been a fox or a dog on a nocturnal prowl, but no, it was too large. My curiosity getting the better of me, I pulled the car into the side of the road, and strained my eyes in an attempt to identify the mysterious animal. I saw another movement, and whatever it was seemed even larger than before. Then I caught my breath, for in the midst of this black moving mass I could discern a whiteness that could only be the snowy background beyond it. What was this mysterious mammal that enabled me to see through it?

All at once I realised that it was not one particular large animal, but a host of smaller ones—rats! *An army of rats was on the move.* Even as I sat and watched, more and more of them were.coming up out of the river, in swift, darting movements, the main bunch behaving as though they were uncertain of their leaders' directions and intentions. Stop, start, stop, start; it was fascinating to watch them. Nearer and nearer they came, as they headed towards the road. I felt shivers running up and down my spine, for I find these creatures revolting in small numbers in broad daylight, but the sight of them moving in an army, beneath a full moon, in the most desolate of places, was in itself both repulsive and frightening. I wound the window up quickly, and as I did so, I heard a low growl from the back seat. My yellow labrador, Remus, was sitting bolt upright, his nose pressed against the glass, his hackles rising. He, too, had seen them, but whether or not he recognised them for what they were I have no idea. He had already defined them as foes, though.

I could easily have driven on, and been well past Clunton, and on towards Aston-on-Clun, before the rats had reached the road. However, I was fascinated, or was it hypnotised? Perhaps I was just curious, for I sat there, silently waiting, wanting a closer view of this rodent army. I put a restraining hand on Remus, for by now his growls were continuous and I wished to remain an unseen spectator.

Now they were coming through the hawthorn hedge, infiltrating on to the road, hesitating at first, as though they were aware that traffic passed along from time to time. They appeared not to see me, nor my car, and for all the concern they showed, I might as well not have been there at all.

The leaders had crossed by now, and were through the opposite hedge, and into the snow-covered fields beyond, followed by the various regiments, scuttling and darting in their wake, oblivious of their destination, as had been their legendary ancestors who had answered the call of the Pied Piper of Hamlyn.

For possibly ten minutes the crossing of the road continued, until finally the last of the stragglers had gone. I confess that I remained there for some time, astounded and revolted by what I had seen. It was as though something was calling them, a call that could not remain unanswered. Whence had they come? The River Clun, the hills beyond, or from over the Welsh border? I do not know. What is more important, what was their intended destination? This is the greatest mystery of all, for, as far as I know, they were neither heard of nor seen again in the vicinity. Some may argue that I had consumed more than the one stated pint of beer, but I, personally, know that I was fully sober at the time. Some time later I was to witness yet another rat movement in a place some seventy miles from this lonely Shropshire road, this time in mid-summer, after a drought which ended in a week of torrential rain. In this particular instant the rodents moved from a river to a nearby canal.

Days later the river flooded its banks in one of the worst deluges on record. Had the rats, somehow, obtained prior knowledge of the impending catastrophy, and sought safety elsewhere? In the case of the Shropshire rat emigration, I can only add that a rapid thaw followed the freeze-up two days later, the River Clun being in full spate, and I leave the reader to draw his own conclusions.

Nevertheless, during my fifteen years of vermin control on my hill-shoot I have shot and trapped very few rats, and tunnels baited with warfarin have gone untouched for long periods. Rats, it would appear, do not favour wooded hills where food is scarce. Instead, they prefer to remain in close proximity to the farms, finding both grain and shelter around the rickyards. It is, therefore, a good idea to encourage the goodwill of these hill farmers by offering to assist them in a ratting foray, using trained ferrets to bolt the quarry which can be dealt with by terriers, sticks, or .410 shotguns. However, a good deal of planning is necessary beforehand if there is to be any measure of success. Safety, of course, is of paramount importance, especially where guns are being used, for once the rats begin to bolt there will be a flurry of activity, with terriers dashing to and fro, and farmhands running forward to deal death blows with sticks and spades to scurrying rats. Often a useful and enjoyable day's sport can be had in this way.

NOTES ON FERRETING AND TRAPPING
FERRETING
The ferret is the animal of the gamekeeper, as explained in the author's book *Ferreting and Trapping for Amateur Gamekeepers*. An invaluable ally, it can be used for both the control of rabbits and rats. Whether the amateur keeper actually keeps ferrets or not, he should be conversant with them for they are an integral part of his job.

However, ferreting in upland regions does present problems which the lowland man seldom meets with. For instance, hedgerows are scarce, and most of the rabbits will have their warrens in almost impenetrable forestry thickets, or clumps of thick gorse which deny access even to the man from the Ministry with his tin of Cymag gas. To add to these difficulties often the ground beneath a thin layer of soil is comprised either of slate or solid rock, rendering the digging out of a lost ferret virtually impossible.

47

KEEPING FERRETS

Ferrets are not the obnoxious creatures which they are reputed to be. If they smell then it is the fault of their owner for housing them badly and not cleaning them out regularly. The hutch should be kept outside in a sheltered place or else in a *dry* outbuilding with ample hay in their bedding quarters. The ferret is a flesh-eating creatures and will be healthiest if confined to a diet of meat. A few rabbits stored in the deep-freeze after a successful foray will enable them to be fed well and cheaply, and fresh water must be available for them at all times. Do not leave uneaten food in the hutch. They should never be allowed to gorge themselves for there is no surer way to kill them.

Pregnant jills can be worked up until a fortnight before giving birth but should be segregated from the other ferrets during this time. Separate quarters should always be available to house these, or those which fall sick. If a number of ferrets are kept then it is a good idea to construct a ferret-court in an outhouse. This consists of a number of separate hutches all opening into a communal forecourt. The animals can be supervised and cleaned out much more easily than having to contend with a number of hutches.

TRAINING YOUNG FERRETS

On their first training session the jill should accompany the ferrets, and if possible try and take them to a warren where there is a likelihood of finding a rabbit. This will serve to encourage them, and let them see what rabbiting is all about. On the second outing, however, it is best to use a warren which is known to be deserted, for now they will be eager to find a rabbit and will explore the tunnels eagerly. Do not prolong the session, however. Like puppies, they must not become bored. Each session must be a novelty.

RABBITING

Often in hill country you will be forced to use a 'liner', a ferret with a cord attached to its collar, and knots tied at intervals of a yard or so in order that you will be able to determine the distance which it has travelled underground. It is unwise to use a muzzle except in the case of a liner, for the creature which remains below ground and you are unable to retrieve, may well starve if it is at large for any length of time.

Top : Foxes on the Vermin Gibbet
Bottom : A Grouse Butt on the Moor

Plate 2

WORKING FERRETS

The rabbits which you intend to try and bolt have their burrows in the heart of a thick belt of coniferous trees, the lowest branches only a yard or so from the ground. Shooting in here will be both impracticable and dangerous so you must rely on purse-nets. Possibly you will have to crawl some fifty yards before you reach the warren. One advantage here is that undergrowth seldom grows beneath these closely-planted trees where the sunlight rarely penetrates, and you should be able to find most of the holes. Move as quietly as possible, placing your nets over the entrances, and then put in your liner. It is best to tie the end of the line to the trunk of a tree, for if it disappears below ground with the ferret it is almost certain to become caught up in the tree roots.

The moment a rabbit bolts and becomes caught up in one of the nets, you must move as quickly as the cramped conditions will allow. The best way of killing a rabbit is with a sharp blow at the base of its skull with the flat of your hand.

Replace the net quickly for it may well be that another rabbit will choose this same hole as an exit.

A calm windless day is best, for you will be able to hear the rabbits moving about below ground. Rabbits are reluctant to bolt in wet weather.

So much for ferreting in thick woodlands. Now let us consider the patch of dense undergrowth, probably a mixture of gorse and bracken, on a steep hillside. In order to locate the holes it may be necessary to cut away some of the obstructing growth. This should be carried out a few days beforehand for it is not a task which can be completed quietly, and the noise involved will encourage the rabbits to remain underground for some time afterwards.

Use a liner again, but this time it is better to shoot rather han to net for your chances of being able to find all the bolt-holes are exceedingly remote. You must judge from the size of the cover how many guns will be necessary. Too many are worse than too few, especially if the patch of undergrowth is completely surrounded. All must be instructed to shoot only after the coneys are past them, and on no account must a shot be taken directly into cover. More than one unfortunate ferret has met its death in this way.

One important factor which must be borne in mind is that rabbits generally prefer to bolt *uphill,* and those guns standing on the upper slopes will get the majority of the shooting.

As with netting, silence is important, and the less talking the better. Do not be in a hurry to move on to another warren when nothing appears to be happening after half-an-hour or so. Many of these hill warrens are extensive, and it may be some time before the rabbits eventually decide to bolt.

Ferreting is not learned in a season. As with everything else it is experience which counts, and it may take several seasons before one is obtaining regular results.

It is unwise to ferret between April and September as most warrens will have nests of young rabbits in them, and much time can be wasted. If one decides not to use a line then the chances are that the ferret ill gorge itself and sleep it off afterwards.

If you have to dig (and it is a lucky man who finds easy digging in the hills), the experience will generally benefit your ferret. The ferret does not like being dug out, and it will learn its lesson. Smoking out ferrets is not advisable. You could well find your animals refusing to go below ground afterwards for some considerable time.

RATS

Rats are a quarry which the hill-shooter will mostly only meet up with around the barns and outbuildings of the hill-farms. There is little to attract them in dense woodlands or barren slopes. Nevertheless, the farmer may well appreciate your efforts to control this, the worst of all vermin, on his land.

Never use young ferrets for ratting. The rat is a vicious creature, and there will be many pitched battles underground. The ferret is the sworn enemy of the rat, and the latter will not relinquish its stronghold readily.

The rules are much the same as for rabbiting except that the action takes place around the farmyard itself. Inspect your ground beforehand, note the holes, block up those in inaccessible places, and determine the weapons and numbers of your 'fighting force', both ferret and human. The more ferrets the better, in fact. Terriers are ideal for dealing with bolting rats, but make sure that these dogs are familiar with ferrets otherwise the casualties could be costly to yourself.

If guns are used, ensure that those shooting are safe shots, and understand ratting. Small guns will be best, either .410s or No. 3-bore

Garden Guns, with perhaps the odd air-rifle to account for those rats which seek safety by scaling walls and sitting on roofs or guttering.

Always carry some TCP to treat those ferrets which are bitten. There is an old saying that a ferret bitten by a rat will die. There is no truth in this, but more likely this belief stems from the fact that in days gone by many of the old rat-catchers seldom went to the trouble of treating these bites.

TRAPPING

An old saying goes that 'a trap never ate anything, it never minded waiting, and it was always at work whilst the keeper was asleep'. This is very true, but the fact remains that *trapping can only be carried out if the traps can be inspected at least once daily*. This means that if you do not live close enough to your shoot, and have the time available to go round your traps daily, then you must either engage someone to carry out this duty for you or else forego it altogether.

Ground vermin such as stoats, weasels, grey squirrels, etc., can seldom resist entering a tunnel when they can see daylight at the other end. Consequently, tunnels placed in *suitable* places will attract these creatures. The best sitings are along stone walls, beside gate-posts, adjacent to streams. These creatures will seldom cross open ground unless forced to do so, and it is in the aforementioned places where you will kill them.

The Fenn Humane Vermin Trap, which replaces the now illegal gin, is probably the best on the market, and is covered in detail in *Ferreting and Trapping for Amateur Gamekeepers*.

Tunnels can be made from three pieces of wood, approximately 3ft long by 6in high and nailed together to form an open-ended rectangular box with the ground as a floor. These are easy to inspect, merely having to be lifted up to see the trap inside, whereas with more elaborate structures constructed of brick and earth much time is wasted in rebuilding each time.

Traps should be set lightly and covered with dead leaves or grass. Soil is likely to obstruct the working mechanism and promote rust. Traps which have not caught chould be sprung and re-set at least once a week. It is best to keep a stock of traps and change them over from time to time. New ones should be allowed to 'weather' before being put into use.

It is a good idea to draw up a detailed plan of your shoot and to mark on it the places most suitable for the siting of traps. Practical experience will soon prove whether your theories are correct. When traps are not catching it is a good idea to change the siting, but leave the empty tunnel in place. Vermin will become used to passing through it without harm, and then, when you start trapping it again, the number of kills will soon mount up.

In hilly areas, unless you have stone walls at your disposal, trapping sites will be more difficult to find. In forestry thickets vermin usually traverse the outskirts, and you may well have to await a fall of snow in order to determine their movements.

WINGED VERMIN TRAPS

It is legal to set net-traps to take those species of birds which are not afforded protection. These can be made from the basic structure of an old gin-trap, the teeth being filed down and replaced with a frame incorporating a net. The extension will need to be welded into place to make it firm, and the plate can be used to attach bait to.

For the purpose of catching crows a 6ft square cage structure can be built with a tapering funnel in the top, and a door by which the trapped birds can be taken out. These are really only effective in the severest of weather, and then only if set in places frequented by corvines. The bait can consist of butchers' scraps, lights, etc., Needless to say, these traps must be visited daily, and those crows which have entered, and find it impossible to fly back up the tunnel, despatched.

RAT-TRAPS

The conventional 'nipper-type' rat-trap is more suited for use around farm buildings. Out on the shoot you will find that your tunnel-traps will account for most of the rats. However, if you have a stream or a flight-pond on your land then it will be advantageous to set a cage-type rat-trap in the vicinity. Catches should be removed as frequently as possible because if the vermin have the opportunity to view their imprisoned colleagues they will soon come to realise that the trap is something to be avoided.

SNARING

It may well be that on particularly dense shoots, where there is little opportunity to ferret rabbit burrows, snaring is the best method. One must learn to determine the rabbit-runs and to set the snares in the correct places. Often it is easier, in those places where Forestry Commission woods are enclosed with mesh-fencing, to seek out the gaps where the coneys pass to and fro, and to use these places. One has the additional advantage of being able to tie the snares to the fence instead of having to drive in stakes.

Snares must be visited at least twice a day, the most important times being shortly after daybreak and just as dusk is turning to darkness. These are the times when rabbits are most active, and once foxes become aware that you are snaring they will learn to search out your snares. Rabbits squeal loudly when first caught, and Reynard will hear them and come to investigate. After his first easy meal he will make a point of inspecting your snares for you!

Trapping and snaring are an enjoyable and worthwhile task. You will be surprised how your shoot will benefit from the carrying out of these duties regularly.

CHAPTER 4

The Hill People and the Seasons

THE HILL-FARMERS

Hill farming is a way of life as opposed to a means by which a living is earned. Over the generations the breed of hill-farmer which we know today has changed very little. His terrain is rugged, and in the bitterest of winters he must still traverse the same treacherous slopes which his forefathers have trodden for centuries searching for missing sheep.

He knows no fixed hours, his day's work commencing with the coming of dawn, and even when darkness has fallen he has jobs to do in the outbuildings, machinery to be maintained, and a host of other chores.

Mostly his farm consists of grazing land, with a few fields of rape or kale to provide winter-feed for his livestock. Seldom is this type of land fertile, even with the liberal use of fresh manure and modern fertilizers. Rocky hillsides are not conducive to agriculture, and mostly cultivation is regarded as self-sufficiency, hay and grain for the cattle in winter, a few vegetables for household use.

His income is derived mainly from sheep, the sale of lambs in the spring, and wool in the early summer. Yet, it is a constant battle against the elements, and the depredations of foxes and crows.

One of the most attractive features of upland agriculture, at once apparent to the visitor to the hills during harvest time, is the sight of fields of stooked corn, something rarely seen in the lowland rural areas, a delight to the eye, a return for many of us to the days of our boyhood.

However, there is a more practical reason for this seemingly primitiveness. It is simply that the narrow winding lanes leading up to these elevated farms are not wide enough to permit the passage of a combine-harvester. It is probable that in fifty years time the old-fashioned binder will still be the primary means of harvesting fields of barley and

4-1 A Typical Hill Farm: A way of life—often tough   (photo: Lance Smith)

rye.

Yet, a modern breed of hill-farmers is emerging, sons who are prepared to accept more modern methods in other ways. Tractors have already replaced the hard working horse on most farms although there is now a positive move to turn back to horses*. Land Rovers have made the task of locating missing sheep much easier, but overall the way of life has not changed. Physical endurance and hard work seven days a week, holidays virtually unknown. This is their life, something which is totally foreign to lowland dwellers.

Only those of us who have cause to visit these hills regularly will appreciate the dedication of these men and their families. It is all team-work, farmers helping each other with total unselfishness, a close-knit community who may give an impression of suspicion and mistrust towards the stranger. Yet this is a barrier which can only be breached by the latter. He must 'prove' himself, and try to understand a mode of existence which is in all probability more sincere than that of the urban dweller where neighbours scarcely pass the time of day with each other.

Many of us work in an unhealthy indoor atmosphere. Our fitness is inferior to theirs as we huddle in our conventionally built townhouses on winter nights, perhaps trying to convince ourselves that we are members of a progressive society. Only a few of us will spare a thought for these hillfarmers, fighting for their very existence against the elements.

Up in the hills the weather is the governing factor, determining the quality of crops, the success of a lambing season, and the standard of living of these unsung heroes. Likewise, the shooting man will discover how severe weather affects his sport. Sometimes it will be to his advantage, whilst on other occasions it will drive his game down into the valleys in search of a warmer climate. There are no fixed rules governing the behaviour of wildlife in hill areas. Birds and beasts seem to come and go according to their own particular fancy.

This only serves to whet the appetite of the hunter. Unpredictability is the spice of life to him.

*See *Great Horses of Britain*. Lee Weatherley, Spur Publications, 1978.

4-2 Winter in the Hills—an idyllic setting for sport   (photo: Lance Smith)

WINTER

Hills are places of beauty at all times of the year. One may have a preference for a certain season. I have one, I know. I appreciate their sheer magnificence for the full twelve months, but I will admit that I do have a special liking for winter. I enjoy the fresh green of early spring, the lush green of summer, and the golden brown of autumn, but there is something about the snowy whiteness of winter that depicts the true splendour and wildness of the place. The changes which man has made to the landscape are buried beneath heavy snowfalls and, apart from the acres of Forestry Commission plantations, we are able to view the scene more or less as our ancestors looked upon it centuries ago.

I will never forget the first fall of snow which I saw in the hills above Clun, many years ago. When I had set out from the industrial midlands, earlier on, it had been a typically damp midwinter's day. It was drizzling by the time I reached Craven Arms, and I foresaw a miserable, wet day ahead of me. However, at Clunton the drizzle turned to sleet, and when I arrived in Clun it was snowing hard. As I began the steep climb up out of Clun I had to resort to the use of fourwheel drive, for the wheels of the Land Rover began to spin in the two inches of snow which covered the narrow lanes.

A blizzard was in full force as I pulled into the gateway leading to my hill-shoot, and I had to wait a full half hour until it abated before I could leave the vehicle. The memory of that first morning will remain with me forever. The skies cleared, and the sun shone out of a cloudless blue sky, sparkling and scintillating on the miles and miles of virgin snow which lay around me. I have seen that view many times since, but nothing can compare with that first morning.

As I moved into the first forestry plantation I heard a cock pheasant in the snowy field which bordered it. It was not the challenging cry of this splendid bird as it rises in defiance of man and dog, but rather a distressed 'cuk-cuk-cuk', the sound which I had been so familiar with in other places where night poaching had been prevalent, and the pheasants had sensed a nocturnal intruder. I stood behind a large oak tree, watching and waiting. Suddenly I saw the pheasant, his splendid colours made all the more beautiful by the whiteness of the background, as he half-ran, half-fluttered, into view over a rise in the ground. I was mystified by his behaviour at first, and then I saw the reason for it as a magnificent dog-fox appeared about fifty yards behind him, hard on his

59

4-3. Setting Off On A Snowy Morning—Be prepared for inclement weather and conditions.

(photo: Lance Smith)

4-4. Times of heavy snowfall mean nothing but hardship for the wildlife of the hills—the gamekeeper must help to ensure survival.

(photo: Lance Smith)

scent. As I watched, my eye caught another movement, then a second, and yet a third. I could hardly believe what I saw, but there was no doubt about it. There were *four* foxes in pursuit of that one pheasant! However, he succeeded in maintaining his lead, and it was not until one of them attempted to cut him off from the nearby woods that he finally resorted to the use of his wings, and with a defiant cackling disappeared over the tops of the spruce thickets.

I have seen a pheasant in a similar predicament several times since, and I cannot understand why this fast flying sporting bird does not take flight at once, and ensure his safety, I know that he prefers to walk rather than fly, as a general rule, but I can only conclude, in these instances, that he revels in the thrill of the chase. It is certainly food for thought.

However, times of heavy snowfall mean nothing but hardship for the wildlife of these border hills. Their natural food supplies are buried beneath deep drifts, and many of the smaller birds die of starvation. It is great satsifaction to myself as I look out of my windows and watch a raging snowstorm to know that on my shoot I have several well-filled "hoppers". Not only will these provide a constant supply of food for game-birds, but they will ensure that such birds as blackbirds, robins and thrushes will find sufficient for their needs. These feeders are very easily made out of a five-gallon drum, with a set of holes bored in the base, and placed on a couple of housebricks. Barley is the best all-round grain to use to suit all species.

One winter, a few years ago, we were fortunate in so much that we had very little snowfall in the hills, or elsewhere, for that matter. However, during one cold spell I came across a green woodpecker, or 'yaffle' as it is sometimes called, which was unable to fly. My yellow labrador, Remus, brought it to me, and I was unable to find any visable damage. I was faced with a problem. To have left it there would have meant certain death from its natural enemies, so I put it in my gamebag, and took it home with me. I was unable to feed it, for this bird finds its food by boring into tree trunks in search of insects. It spent the night in a cardboard box close to a central-heating radiator, and the following morning I took it to a gamekeeper friend of mine whose estate was far from the bird's native border hills. There was no snow lying here, and it was a warm day for the time of year as I released it in some rhododendron bushes close to the keeper's cottage. It recovered its powers of flight within a few hours, and my friend saw it in the vicinity

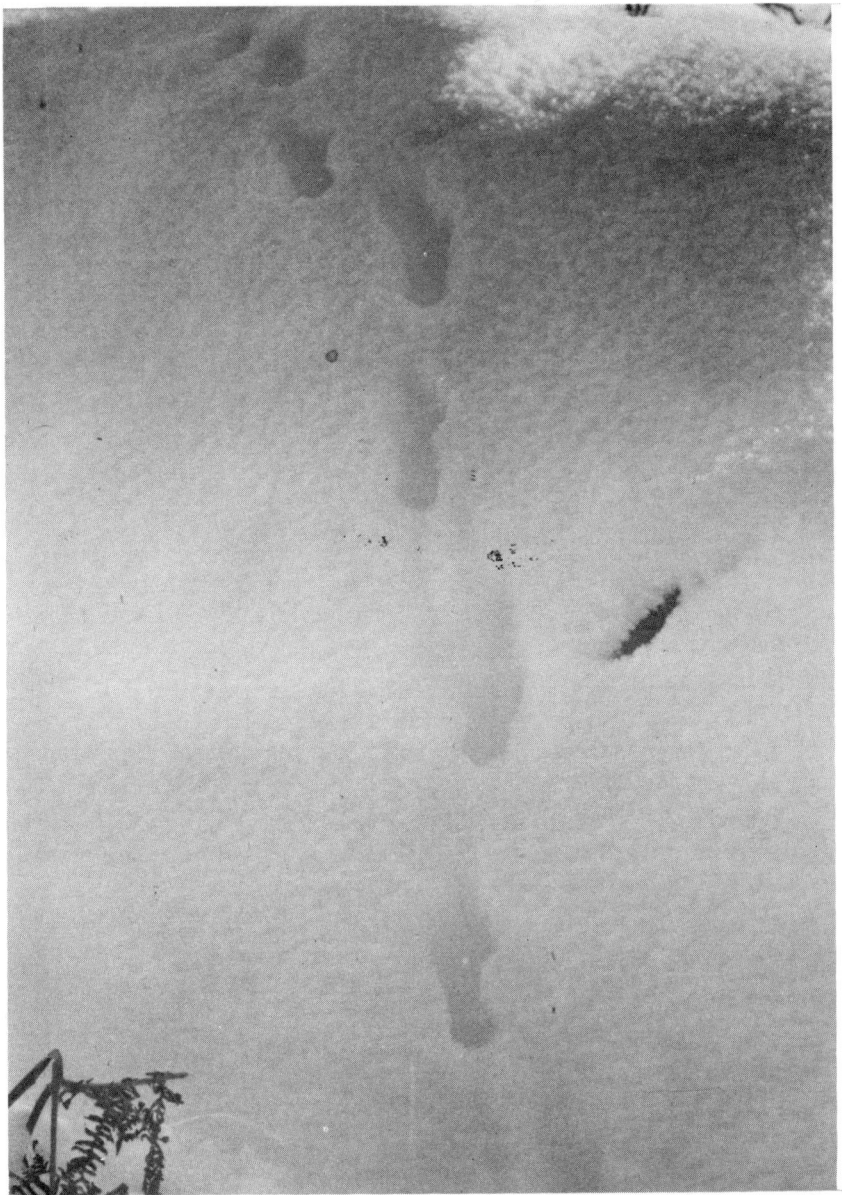

4-5. Rabbit tracks in the snow—tracking is easy but conditions restrict movement.

(photo: Lance Smith)

for some weeks afterwards, until it finally disappeared. I was happy that I had saved its life, but my only regret was that I had been unable to return it to its former home in the hills.

Wintertime in the hills is not a time to relax. There is much work to be done for the man who is interested in the countryside, and there is great satisfaction to be gained from the knowledge that one has helped both birds and beasts to survive a severe spell of weather. I love the snowy months, but I do not intend merely to view them through the window whilst enjoying the comfort of a centrally-heated room.

SHOOTING IN SNOW AND RAIN

Snow exhilarates, rain depresses. I heard this statement from a well-known sportsman a long time ago, and many times since I have been reminded of it, realising only too well how aptly he had summed up weather conditions in relation to shooting.

I am one of those shooting men who, foolishly perhaps, sets forth with a gun and dog, regardless of the elements. During the year, I inevitably shoot in snow, rain, fog and sunshine, the latter, of course, being the most comfortable. However, I have had more than my share of the first two, and I find that they have exactly the opposite effects upon my general disposition.

It is frustrating, to say the least, after a week of fine, sunny days, to awake on Saturday morning to the sound of rain lashing at the windows. One's natural inclination is to groan, turn over in bed, and go to sleep again. However, realising that if I succumb to this temptation, I may not have the chance of a shot until the following week, and, even then, there might be similar conditions to contend with, I arise and don my waterproofs. Usually, in this type of weather, I wear thigh-length waders even for game-shooting, for I consider that the tiredness brought about at the end of the day, through this, far outweighs the discomfort of spending several hours in soaking wet trousers. The reader will at once wonder why I do not invest in a pair of waterproof trousers, but I find that these cause my legs to perspire to such a degree that I am faced with the decision of whether it is better to become wet inside or out. Probably I shall reverse my opinion in later years!

Rain is by no means an incentive to shoot well. Freedom of movement is somewhat restricted by the unaccustomed stiffness of waterproof clothing, and birds and beasts are reluctant to move unless absolutely

64

compelled to do so by a dog whose enthusiasm leaves much to be desired. Many organised shoots are apt to cancel the day's proceedings if the inclement weather does not look like relenting before midday. Beaters will, naturally, shirk the thickest cover, and often a field of tall kale will be ignored by a sympathetic host. An early finish will be uppermost in the minds of those who have persevered, and a small bag will be inevitable.

I can only recall one really successful day in wet weather, and it took place whilst I was a guest at a hill-shoot very similar to my own some years ago. Saturated and dejected, eight of us had walked all day in driving rain. Of our host's hand-reared pheasants there was no sign, and apart from a few rabbits and a hare, it seemed that it was going to be one of the blankest days on record. Five acres of kale remained, and we kept trying to convince ourselves that nothing would be found in such soaking wet cover. However, at the very end of the day we decided that we could not possibly become any wetter, so we plunged into this uninviting cover. Five minutes later, pheasants were striking up everywhere, and we finished the day on a triumphant note, killing something like twenty out of the sixty or so flushed.

On another day, two of us had driven seventy miles to my own shoot, and just as we arrived, the heavens opened in one of the worst downpours which I have ever witnessed. We sat in the car for over an hour, but as it showed no signs of abating, we decided on a quick walk through an adjacent field of rape, more in an attempt to console ourselves for the waste of four gallons of petrol. We were out for only twenty minutes in those dreadful conditions, and during that short space of time we accounted for a brace of pheasants, two hares and a rabbit! Very seldom does one conclude such days with anything approaching any degree of satisfaction.

Now, snow is a different propostion altogether. Provided that there is only a light covering, enabling one to traverse the fields and coverts reasonably comfortably, one could not wish for better conditions. The "Christmas Card" scenery is pleasing to the eye, and both fur and feather will be abroad in search of food. Furthermore, the observant and interested sportsman will be able to ascertain from the tracks in the fresh snow what game and vermin he has on his land, and which are their favourite haunts. Fairly warm clothing will be called for, but those impeding waterproofs can be left at home. What can be a more congenial setting than such a morning, with the sun shining out of a cloudless blue sky, and a chance of meeting up with a splendidly plumaged cock pheasant in the fir-woods, or a mallard on the brook which runs behind it?

During the days when I possessed a Land Rover, even a heavy overnight fall of snow did not deter me from visiting my beloved hills. Many an arduous journey, the final climb up through the narrow winding lanes completed in four-wheel drive, saw me at the entrance to my shoot, with deep snow drifts all around me. Full of anticipation, I would set out, floundering up to my waist at times in the powdery white substance, and, more often than not, I would not see a sign of life on the whole of my 600 acres.

This illustrates the difference between a light and a heavy fall of snow, particularly on high ground. The former serves to encourage wildlife to move about, whilst the latter either drives them down the valleys to a slightly warmer climate, or encourages them to take advantage of the shelter of the deep woods.

Of course, the pigeon-shooter will be in his element with the advent of snow, particularly if he has access to a field of greenstuff. Large bags can be made over decoys in these places, although the birds shot will hardly be fit for human consumption, their flesh bitter after a diet of cabbage or kale, with precious little meat on them if there has been a prolonged spell of this type of weather. My shooting companion once shot 300 woodpigeons during the hard winter of 1962/63, and not a single bird was fit for the table.

A TIME FOR EXTRA SAFETY

Shooting in snow calls for the greatest attention to safety. A blocked barrel can result in a serious burst, and a slip on a frozen surface can have the direst consequences in a variety of mishaps. Caution has always been uppermost in my mind ever since a man who lived not far from me, a long time ago, set off after duck on a flooded water-meadow, one moonlight night, when a deep snow lay over the surrounding countryside. Somehow, he lost his footing when crossing a stile, grabbed at his falling gun by the barrels, and shot himself. A terrible tragedy, and such an unnecessary waste of life.

A fall of snow is always irresistible to me. I find myself automatically preparing for a foray. My yellow labrador is equally fired with this wintry enthusiasm, and my wife constantly mutters something about "mad dogs and shooting men . . .!"

A HERON AND A PARROT

I have already mentioned the unpredictable ways in which wildlife are inclined to react during spells of hard weather. Yet few could be as unique as the incident which occurred during the winter of 1972/73. That winter we experienced one of the heaviest snowfalls which we have had in the Midlands for the past four or five years. It was the unexpectedness of it which made it all the more remarkable, for there was no hint of it after daylight on the Friday morning, in spite of the leaden skies, which even the experts had foretold as impending heavy rain, yet, by 11 a.m. a veritable blizzard was raging. It did not relent for the next six hours, and the wisdom of abandoning my weekly shooting expedition to the hills had already occurred to me. However, with a thaw in progress by 8 p.m., I decided to go ahead with my usual plans.

The following morning I was already regretting my decision as the car slithered and skidded through the snowbound lanes in the hills. The surface was one of packed frozen snow, on which the belt of incoming milder weather had not yet had time to make any impression. Consequently, I was fortunate to reach one of the lower farms on my shoot, and, on Farmer Roberts' advice, I decided to leave my car there, and plan my foray from this point.

The expidition itself was, to say the least, a waste of time. As so often happens, in this part of the world, at the advent of hard weather the majority of the wildlife seems to desert the area, and head for the valleys in search of food and shelter. The sun shone out of a cloudless blue sky onto a dazzling white fairyland all day, yet nowhere was there so much as a woodpigeon to be seen. Remus, my yellow labrador sniffed hopefully at a few fresh rabbit tracks, and on occasions we caught the unmistakable odour of Reynard in the fresh breeze, but not once did we glimpse even a movement in the snow covered undergrowth.

The sun was sinking behind the western, snow-capped mountains, when I arrived back in the farmyard, my barrels as clean as when I had set out. The farmer was awaiting my return, stamping his feet in the snow, and rubbing his hands together in an attempt to keep warm. I have always realised the importance of being prepared to spend a few minutes chatting to these hardy hill-folk, for their knowledge of the

67

countryside is limitless, and, apart from that, their goodwill is of the greatest help to such as myself, whose visits are too brief to accumulate anything approaching their own experience.

"Quite a week we've had this week," he told me, as I began changing my boots and putting away my gun. "Mr. Olton, down at the next farm 'as lost 'is parrot. 'Ad it almost twenty years, 'e 'as. Never needed a cage for it, either. Then, Tuesday mornin', it took it into its 'ead to fly off up the 'dingle'. 'Asn't been seen since. What with this weather, though, I'm afraid it's 'ad it. We shan't see Polly agin!"

He persuaded me to partake of some of his wife's home-made cake and a cup of tea, in the large kitchen, and then, as we stepped outside again, dusk was already falling. Whilst we stood there, still chatting, I caught a movement in the darkening sky above the farmhouse and, on looking up, my first thought was that a prehistoric pterodactyl was swooping down upon us. It had a wingspan of some 4/5ft., a tiny body, and a long, wicked-looking bill.

"A heron!" I gasped, recognition and reality registering on my brain.

"And it's coming down," Farmer Roberts added.

So it was. It alighted daintily on the snow-covered sheep-field, some fifty yards from where we stood, and remained stationary, like some garden statue. The remarkable fact about the whole episode was that there was no water within at least a radius of a mile.

Roberts was already clambering over the gate, and walking towards it. I followed him, though I knew not why, for our chance of getting within twenty yards of this, one of the wariest of birds, was remote, and, even if we managed this, I had no wish to come within striking distance of that reputedly razor-sharp bill.

However, it remained there, until my farmer friend was less than ten yards from it, when, with an almost casual flap of those mighty wings, it became airborne again. We stood watching, expecting it to disappear into the rapidly thickening gloom, but, less than thirty yards further on, it alighted again.

"Now, what d'you make o' that?" Roberts had pushed his tattered cap on to the back of his head, and was scratching his mop of unruly grey hair in bewilderment.

However, I was not paying attention to his perplexity, for something else had caught my eye. Amongst the snowy boughs of a stunted fir tree, barely six feet above the ground, I caught a glimpse of something red and green. I stared at it intently, and was just able to make out the form of a brightly coloured bird, about the size of a fully grown carrion crow.

"There," I was pointing, "In that tree . . ."

"Ah!" a long sigh escaped the farmer's lips. "Reg Olton's parrot! Here, Polly, good girl . . ."

There was no fear of the parrot escaping. It was too bedraggled and crestfallen. It gave no trouble as my companion reached up, and caught hold of it. In fact, it almost seemed relieved to see us.

This latest diversion caused us to forget completely the 'tame' heron which had initially led us up the field. Our priority was to take this exotic looking bird indoors to the warmth of a blazing log-fire, and when, eventually, our thoughts returned to the heron, it was too dark to see it, anyway.

Polly made a remarkable recovery, I am pleased to say, though how she had survived four days, exposed to the elements, is beyond me. As for that heron, it was never seen again. Undoubtedly, it saved Farmer Olton's 'Polly' by its uncharacteristic behaviour, but why should it suddenly decide to alight on a snow-covered sheep-field with no water, whatsoever in the vicinity? I can only conclude that the truant-playing Polly was the direct cause. Perhaps the heron, spotting it sheltering in the fir tree, regarded it as a foe, and, although not an aggressive bird by nature, had decided to challenge it. Or, maybe, it was just curious. Whatever the answer to this, another of Nature's mysteries, we shall never really know for certain.

SUMMER

There are far too many tenants who neglect their shooting rights almost completely between February 1st and September 1st. Apart from the obvious keepering duties, however, basic, there is another way in which one may take full advantage of the facilities at one's disposal. Having established a relationship with the hill-farming fraternity, it is wrong to overlook family and friends who remain at home during those autumnal and winter shooting days which afford the sportsman so much pleasure.

During the close season I think that it is always a good idea if the tenant of a shoot invites his own family, and/or those of friends who regularly shoot with him, to spend a day on the land in question. Most families, particularly those from urban areas, will welcome the oppor-tunity of a day out in the countryside, particularly in a secluded place where they will not be surrounded by litter or pestered by fellow picnickers.

It is only right that a "shooting widow" should have a mental picture of the place to which her husband disappears on those frequent weekends between September and February. Likewise, it is giving the children an early insight into the sport which their father so fanatically pursues. If the shoot is a long way from home, and they live in a large town or city, then they may never be given the chance to acquaint themselves with a worthy sport and outdoor life. Youngsters are very impressionable, and if their father never gives them an opportunity to see for themselves what goes on on a shoot, then they may follow instead in the footsteps of older boys in their own neighbourhood, and settle for some such pastime as disturbing the peace and endangering the lives of pedestrians by roaring round the streets on powerful motorbikes, little knowing what other more worthwhile joys they are missing.

One summer weekend I took a friend and his wife, and his two young boys aged five and three, down to my hill shoot in Shropshire for the day. The sun shone and all was serene, the panoramic view at its best. We shared a delightful picnic lunch on the "shores" of my flight-pond, and during the afternoon enjoyed a long walk around the thick forestry plantations. This was followed by tea in the shelter of some large oak trees, for in this part of the world the evenings are invariably cool. It was a wonderful day, thoroughly enjoyed by all, and I must confess that it provided me with as much pleasure, unfolding the mysteries of shooting to this friend's family, as I normally obtain from a good day in the height of the season. Naturally, the youngsters were not old enough to understand fully what it was really all about, but the important thing was that the seeds had been sown. It will be a memory that will remain with them until they are ready to have a gun of their own. Already their toy pop-guns have another meaning in their lives besides imitating their cowboy heroes which they watch regularly on their television screens.

I think it is essential for the peace of mind of a wife to know the type of terrain which her husband visits regularly. All too often the national press report wildfowling and other shooting accidents, totally exaggerating the dangers of marshland and ground on which the tragedy occurred. I will admit that there are dangerous tracts of hill country and marshes where an accident could prove fatal, but more often than not

70

the fault lies with the people involved. Likewise, a man who scales a steep rocky slope with a loaded gun, probably not even on "safe", and suffers a serious or even fatal fall as a result will succeed in getting that particular piece of land adverse publicity which is totally unfounded. The wife of a shooting man who has never set foot on his shoot may imagine all kinds of dangers which her husband may be facing weekly. However, once she has assured herself that he shoots over a tract of "normal" countryside, with no treacherous quicksands or sheer cliffs to endanger his life, then she will remain at home with peace of mind, and her close season visit to the shoot will have been justified.

Those shooting men who are content only to visit their land during the winter months, are allowing the vermin and trespassers to gain the upper hand. Most men will explain, when confronted with this argument, that their wives and families expect to be taken out for long runs in the car at weekends during the summer months. One cannot blame him for this, but if he were to take his family down to the shoot regularly, and get them interested in it, then he would be fulfilling both halves of his obligation. It is amazing the interest which a wife will show in a shoot if she feels that she is part of it, and playing a role in it. She is walking and picnicking where others have no right to be, and she is privileged in this respect. At the same time by being there she is enabling her husband to keeper and improve his shoot. This means there will probably be more game for the larder next season, and she will be able to save that little bit extra out of the housekeeping towards a new coat or dress. Whilst her husband is over the fields pursuing carrion crows or grey squirrels, she can occupy her time picking bilberries or blackberries, according to the time of year, or gathering some firewood. There are a hundred and one little interesting tasks with which she can occupy herself to while away the time.

I would strongly advise, however, the shooting man who is contemplating introducing his family to his shoot, to listen to the weather forecasts very carefully for the first two or three times anyway. Nothing can be more depressing for a family than to arrive at some spot, miles away from the nearest town, only to find that the view is obscured by low cloud, and it is pouring with rain. A first visit under these circumstances could be disastrous, and the unfortunate shooting tenant may well find himself joining traffic queues heading for the coast on the following weekend when the sun has decided to shine.

71

I think that all shoots, whether syndicate or rough-shoots, should be a●family affair. They are a pleasure to be shared, and problems and new ideas can be discussed by all at home. A man will pursue his chosen sport with far more success if he feels that he has the support of his family rather than if he has to set off for his shoot at weekends feeling that he is deserting them for his won selfish pleasure.

LEARNING TO FORECAST THE WEATHER

The majority of hill-folk, whom we have already discussed in this chapter, have learnt the knack of weather-forecasting with reasonable accuracy. There is nothing magical about this 'gift'. Mostly it is a case of simple observation, something which the shooting man is quite capable of carrying out for himself. There are limitations, of course, but even a scanty knowledge of that which the elements have in store for us are helpful in the organisation of a day's shooting, particularly in the hills where conditions change so drastically, sunshine one minute, a torrential downpour the next.

Weather-forecasting is an interesting, if not always successful, hobby. Using a few simple observations it is a challenge to the countryman to see if he can beat the experts from the meteorological office, and it will afford him a great deal of satisfaction if his sunshine turns up in place of the weatherman's wind and rain.

A barometer must be looked upon as a guide, and cannot be relied upon implicitly. It is not solely a case of whether the needle goes up or down, but the speed at which it does this. It can only forecast as far as the imminent future, perhaps three or four hours ahead. For instance, during a spell of fine weather, if this instrument is observed to be rising very slowly, then there is every indication that the weather will continue, more so if the wind is in the north, and the atmosphere is dry. However, a damp atmosphere could mean rain in spite of the rise. A rising barometer in the dead of winter is one of the surest signs that snow is on the way.

However, there are other natural signs which, read with intelligence and taken into account along with other factors, can assist one in forecasting the weather that lies ahead. For instance a haze or ring around the moon is a sign of wet weather. The old sayings, "A red sky at night is a shepherd's delight" and "A red sky in the morning is a shepherd's warning" are not to be taken literally, for more often than not I have known them to mean the reverse. The atmosphere must be taken into consideration when applying these age-old sayings. Cloud formation, also, can tell the keen observer much. A large amount of cirrus is a warning that rough weather is on the way, whilst a "mackerel" sky is a good sign, and when this latter is noticed during a warm spell it is a fair indication that the present situation will remain unchanged for a day or two, anyway. The "cotton wool" clouds, those puffs of white cloud in a deep blue summer's sky, are also a good sign.

During a wet day, when there has been incessant pouring rain for hours on end, and then one suddenly notices that the sky is clearing in the form of an arc on the horizon, one can safely say that a change for the better is on the way. Likewise, a cloudy sky will very often clear at moonrise, particularly during the period when the moon is full.

Other signs to watch for are amongst the wild flowers. A poppy, for example, will partially close its petals when rain is imminent. Butterflies will be found inside the heads of flowers rather than perched on top of them, and cattle will be seeking the shelter of a surrounding hedgerow long before the rain arrives.

During a fine spell in the summer months, I always look to see whether there is a misty haze over the distant landscape, about an hour before darkness is due to fall. If there is one, then one can safely bet that the weather will remain settled on the morrow. However, if everywhere is clear, without the slightest trace of mist, then this is a warning, all the more so if there is a wind getting up.

Some years ago I bought a small novelty weather house. This operated by means of a length of gut which contracts in dry weather and expands in wet weather, thus allowing either the "master" or the "lady" of the house to appear in the doorway. It works well, but it is not a forecaster. It merely informs one of the present weather conditions.

A more reliable guide to weather prospects is a bunch of homegrown tobacco leaves hung in a sheltered, but not enclosed, place. These leaves are very sensitive to atmospheric conditions, and will give one a few hours warning by becoming moist for wet weather, but it usually takes an hour or two of fine weather to dry them out again, so they are really only a guide to rain. I have heard that a bunch of hops can be put to similar use. Attempting "long-range" weather forecasts is a waste of time, for such interpretations of a bad winter by an abundance of berries, means absolutely nothing. I have known the mildest of winters after the hedges and bushes have been loaded with berries. One must be content with the morrow only.

In this modern day and age it is only too easy to tune in to a television or radio weather forecast, and be able to receive a regionalised report as well, but a great deal more satisfaction can be gained by taking all the relative factors into consideration, and attempting to forecast the prospects for the following day. The only drawback is that one is inclined to be biased when a day at the sea or in the country is planned, and then one is apt to read all the signs favourably.

HILL FOGS

THE DANGERS

Hill fogs are apt to form at any time of the year, and come down almost without warning. Whilst the danger of becoming lost is not so serious as it is on the marshes where the wildfowler could well find himself cut off by an incoming tide, the prospect of spending a night wandering about in the hills is not a pleasant one. Also, on very rugged terrain, one runs the risk of falling from a narrow sheep-track and possibly suffering injury.

If you are unfamiliar with the particular area, it is wise to carry a compass, but you must determine how to use it before setting out. It is no good carrying this instrument in your pocket, and then, as a belt of low cloud obscures all the landmarks, trying to get your bearings. Practise with the compass in clear weather, take your bearings, and you have the assurance then that at least you will be heading back towards your parked vehicle.

Signal flares, as carried by wildfowlers, are not much use in remote upland areas, simply because there is little likelihood of there being anybody about to see them. *However, a torch is a must.* A small one that fits easily into your pocket will suffice, and will be useful, not only in fog, but on those occasions when you have stopped late in a place far from your car to wait for pigeons. You are just as likely to fall over a small precipice in the dark as you are in fog.

In dull rainy weather there is always the chance of fog developing towards nightfall. In these cases it is wisest to curtail your sport and head for home.

Sometimes fogs will persist for days on end, and when this happens one's sport will suffer. Pigeons will prefer to roost in woods lower down, and wild duck will not come in search of your well-fed pool.

SHOOTING IN THE FOG

A sudden fog can, however, provide an opportunity to make a reasonable bag of woodpigeons. Those birds which are already in the woods when the fog descends will remain there, merely flying short distances when disturbed. The sound of one's shots will also be blanketed to some extent, and whereas in clear conditions a couple of barrels will ensure that every woodie leaves the thickets, in fog they will remain. Certainly this is not as sporting as shooting under normal conditions, but the number killed will be that much greater.

THE UTMOST SAFETY PRECAUTIONS ARE NECESSARY

As far as any form of game shooting is concerned, fog can present a real hazard when more than a couple of guns are present. The author remembers one occasion whilst grouse shooting in Scotland when a sudden mist came down over the high moors. There were a dozen or so guns in all, and the greatest problem was in maintaining a straight line. This was eventually overcome by making certain that each gun could see his neighbour on either side, and reducing the distance between each sportsman. The only drawback was that it was too dangerous to have a forward flank gun on either side, and as a result of this one or two coveys departed unshot at. Much of the day was spoilt by being deprived of the splendid panoramic views which are always an integral part of the true sportsman's day. It was a colourless, characterless day with a very small head of birds killed at the end of it.

Under no circumstances should any attempt be made to drive birds towards waiting guns. Beaters and shooters will not be able to see each other, and there is a very real danger of someone getting shot.

DIFFICULTY IN IDENTIFYING ONE'S QUARRY

One's legitimate quarry is not always easily identifiable in thick fog. This fact was once brought home to the author some years ago when he was instructing a young friend in the art of shooting. A thick fog descended sometime after mid-day, but it was decided to persevere for another hour or so. Suddenly, this young sportsman stopped, peering at something in the ride ahead, some twenty yards away, barely recognisable. Next moment he had mounted his gun and fired.

75

"A rabbit!" he shouted in glee, running forward to retrieve his kill.

It was no rabbit, though. It was a *woodcock* which had been foraging for food amongst the dead leaves! It could have been worse. That hasty shot could have accounted for a green woodpecker, a plover, or any other form of protected wildlife.

Another point worth mentioning here is that all shots taken in fog should be at an angle of no less than 45 degrees. You may not be the only person abroad in such conditions. There are forestry workers, shepherds, ramblers, and a host of other people who might decide to brave the elements. There is no knowing what lies behind that grey wall of opaqueness.

Fog is not good for one's health, particularly the bronchial sufferer. There is little enjoyment to be gained from this type of weather, and apart from the odd chance of making a bag of woodpigeons, the shooter would be well advised to conserve his energy for a more congenial day.

CHAPTER 5

Overall Fitness and Gamekeeping

A QUESTION OF FITNESS

When the word "fitness" crops up in sporting circles, this automatically conjures up pictures of athletes, and of sports requiring a fair amount of physical exertion. However, one's physical condition, to a somewhat lesser extent, is as important with regard to shooting as it is in other outdoor pursuits, and particularly so in the case of the hill-shooter.

Where driven game is concerned, it is usually the older members of the party who occupy a constant position in the line of waiting guns whilst the younger and fitter ones take it in turns to walk with the beaters, thereby enabling some of the birds, which inevitably break back, to be dealt with. However, it is imperative that he who relies on others to drive his game to him is *reasonably* fit also. He must be able to withstand the cold to some extent, for a drive can take up to an hour or more, depending on how far away the beaters have started from. It is no good relying on extra woollen garments for warmth, because this is the surest way to encumber the freedom of movement so necessary for good shooting. Likewise, whilst an odd nip at a pocket flask may be excusable and beneficial in moderation, an excess of alcohol in the bloodstream is as dangerous in the shooting field as it is on the road.

Where a full day's shooting is contemplated, a good breakfast beforehand is essential, particularly in cold weather. I realised the importance of this one Boxing Day, some years ago, whilst shooting in the company of an elderly gentleman and a young friend. It was to be a casual walk through woodlands for the three of us during the morning, followed by a foray after duck in the afternoon.

As we started out, soon after nine o'clock that morning, the cold was intense. There had been a hard frost for the past three days, and the temperature showed no signs of relenting. All went well for the first hour, although I had noticed that the complexion of our elderly friend had become a deep purple. I dismissed the matter from my mind, but ten minutes later it was brought back to me with a jolt as he collapsed unconscious into the thick bracken.

Leaving my young companion to look after him to the best of his ability, I shed my shooting jacket and other cumbersome gear, and began a two-mile cross-country run to the nearest house. Having summoned an ambulance, I then ran back to the entrance to the woods, in order to await its arrival, and guide the men to the scene of the truble. Ten minutes later I was seated between the two uniformed men as the driver slowly edged the vehicle down a wide bridle path.

Imagine my relief and surprise when we met my two colleagues, *walking* up the track towards us. The invalid had apparently made a rapid recovery, although he was considerably shaken. I felt rather embarrassed, however, fearing lest the two ambulance men should think that I had played a practical joke on them, but they were quite understanding, insisting, though, that they carried out an examination of the "patient" there and then. This they did, and explained that there was no cause for worry whatsoever. The incident had been brought about entirely by this gentleman setting out on a bitterly cold morning, having had very little to eat beforehand, and this alone had caused him to collapse and alarm both of us. A lesson was learned there and then, and since that day I have always made sure that I have had sufficient nourishment prior to a day's shooting. Incidentially, I find cereals, with either honey or syrup, to be the most sustaining food of all.

Excess weight is another danger to the rough-shooter who is forced to walk long distances over steep countryside in search of his sport. I remember one day, shooting in the company of a young man who weighed all of 16 stone, but appeared to be quite healthy with it. During the course of the day we beat out a particularly steep slope of a valley, being forced to make the return journey uphill, forcing our way through thick gorse and blackberry bushes. By the time we reached the road at the top, my friend had turned a very sickly shade of grey, and was finding difficulty in breathing. As a result he had to lie down in the heather for a full half hour before he was able to progress any further. I felt guilty, in some respects, in subjecting him to these rigorous conditions, but I had not then fully realised the disadvantages of being overweight.

Having learnt from past experience, I am now very particular about what type of walking I subject any of my guests to on my hill-shoot, carefully bearing in mind their age and physical condition. I am fortunate in having a network of Forestry Commission roads through my shoot, giving me easy access with a vehicle. This means that I can transport certain guests to various areas which I intend to work through, without tiring them unnecessarily with a long walk.

I think one of the greatest dangers which shooters, who are not in the best of health, subject themselves to is when they accept invitations to semi-organised shoots where walking-up is the order of the day. I have attended several of these over the years, and the type I refer to are those on which about twenty guns have been invited to shoot over possibly no more than a couple of hundred acres. I have vivid memories of one of these, when the line of guns and beaters, supposedly walking a field from end to end, stretched diagonally across it. The robust were forging eagery ahead, whilst the older members of the party were puffing along way behind in a vain attempt to keep up. The partridges were the only ones to gain from this disorganised day's shooting, for covey after covey escaped completely unscathed. I had another similar instance whilst grouse shooting on the Scottish moors. The line of guns, which stretched for possibly half a mile, became chaotic, due to odd patches of marshy bogs amongst the heather. Those on firm ground selfishly refused to wait for the unfortunate ones who found themselves floundering, and two or three elderly men were forced to drop behind, finding the high altitude too much for them. Strange to relate, one of our party was a young man weighing no less than 20 stone, and it was he who led the field for most of the day! His enthusiasm knew no bounds, but I feel sure that he must be one of the few men of this weight capable of maintaining such a consistent standard of walking.

A man must shoot accordingly to his physical capabilities. Those who are elderly or not in good health will be much happier pottering round the hedgerows at their own speed, and will enjoy themselves far more than by trying to keep up with a party of younger men whose intention it is to cover the maximum amount of ground possible in a day. This man may well enjoy more sport this way, for I am fully convinced that much game is often walked over where any degree of swiftness is maintained. It is far better to be slow and sure.

GAMEKEEPING

Those of us nowadays who are fortunate enough to be able to rent our own shoot, however small it may be, are in a very enviable position. Some, perhaps, may take it for granted, treating it as somewhere to pass a few pleasant hours during the winter months, and then forget that it even exists between February and September. Alas, there are far too many small shooting tenants today who adopt this attituds, and it is nothing short of wasteful. They simply are not getting what they are paying for, and the old excuse that a place is better kept quiet during the close season simply doesn't hold water. The solution to the problem is not to be found in staying away, for in this way, unless one has a part-time keeper, the gate is merely being opened for picnickers and trespassers of all descriptions.

February 1st is not the date on which one carefully oils one's gun, and puts it safely away for the next few months. Agreed, game and wildfowl shooting has now come to an end, but almost every shoot has a few pigeons to offer for the following six weeks, and, in many areas, rabbits as well. However, pleasurable as sport with the humble woodie and coney may be, once April arrives it is time for *work*. The less dedicated amongst us will certainly turn either to clay-pigeon shooting or some recreation far removed from game preservation. Every man to his liking, but I personally would not anticipate the coming shooting season with such eagerness had I not taken steps, however insignificant, in an attempt to improve a meagre stock of wild pheasant or duck. I would feel the same as I would if I was running a car, and disregarding regular servicing and maintenance.

I am referring, of course, to the man who rents or owns a shoot, and has a minimum amount of time available in which to look after it. The dedicated amateur keeper, naturally, will spend virtually every spare minute of his time, apart from sleeping, on his shoot. In most cases this latter type will rear a few pheasants or duck to supplement his wild birds, and will be entitled to expect better results than his neighbour who relies solely upon Nature.

Vermin-control is probably the most important factor to which it will pay the busy man to devote most of the time which he has to spare. Tunnel-trapping is quite out of the question on account of the necessary regularity of looking at the traps. Therefore he must rely solely upon his gun. A rifle is preferable, if a Firearm's Certificate can be obtained from

5-1. Carrion Crow on the Sheep Fields.

(photo: Calvin Williams)

the police, for its report will be negligible when compared with that of a shotgun. Nesting game will not be disturbed, and neither, for that matter, will one's quarry. A pair of carrion crows can be accounted for at roost without the second bird being put off by the sound of the shot. However, even if a shotgun has to be used, then the disturbance involved will more than compensate for that carrion which would otherwise still be free to pillage the nests of pheasants and partridge.

Crows head my "wanted" list, followed closely by jays, magpies, rats, and grey squirrels. I rate these as far more of a menance than stoats and weasels, for they are definite egg-hunters, whereas the latter will only plunder a nest if they happen to come across one.

February, with snow lying on the ground, is the ideal time to wage war on the corvine tribe. The keeper, full or part-time, will probably build himself a large cagetrap in which to take these birds in numbers. However, decoys, preferably used in conjunction with a rubber or stuffed owl, and a crow-call, should suffice, and in hard weather when these villains are less wary (!), it is possible to make a bag running into double figures. Every corvine killed now may well mean a nest saved in the coming spring.

Next to vermin-control, regular feeding on the rough shoot is one way of ensuring at least a very small number of birds. By this I do not mean enticing a neighbour's pheasants over the boundary, or shooting duck indiscriminately, which have chanced to find your previously neglected flight-pond. Hoppers are invaluable where time does not permit regular daily feeding of the coverts. The only drawback here is that feeders of this type attract rats, and it is essential to use the type whereby the feed falls to the ground in small quantities as the birds peck at it. Grain which lies on the ground for any leagth of time will either go mouldy or begin to sprout, as well as encouraging vermin to feed there.

As the summer passes, one experiences that thrill of anticipation known only to the shooting man. The days are already shortening, and that 'nip' in the air in the evenings heralds the whisper of magical wingbeats in the gathering dusk, and the whistle of teal when winter finally arrives. The splendid cock pheasant will strut across a carpet of golden leaves in the late autumnal sunshine, and a covey of partridges will 'whirr' up out of the last remaining patch of stubble which has yet to come under the plough. Deep down inside one there will be that feeling of satisfaction in the knowledge of a job well done. Perhaps if one had not shot that Carrion Crow which was nesting in the old spinny then there would only have been half a dozen birds in that covey of partridges, or the whole brood might have been wiped out. Who knows? On looking round one's 'estate' one might be forgiven for feeling somewhat self-satisfied. The knowledge that one has done one's share, however small, is reward enough in itself.

In the hills each man is his own keeper. Yet, there are times when, regrettably, these duties have to be reduced to a minimum, especially on Forestry Commission shoots where timber must take priority.

WHEN FORESTRY WORK AND CONSERVATION CLASH

For one whole year I was prevented from doing any keepering on my hill-shoot. Before the reader hastily dismisses me as a lazy, pot-hunting type, out to bag as much as possible with the minimum amount of effort, I would ask him to bear with me whilst I explain the reasons for my apparent negligence.

As most tenants of Forestry Commission shoots are aware, one can enjoy several years of troublefree sport, often never catching sight of a soul, except perhaps the beat-forester paying a cursory visit, from time to time, and then, suddenly, the whole position can change overnight. The plantations of conifers, which have been growing steadily all the time, are now ready for brashing and thinning, the mature ones for felling, and before you know what is happening your quiet refuge has been invaded by teams of contract-workers, heavy lorries, and all the various equipment necessary to complete the job. The tranquility is shattered by the constant whine of chainsaws, and a general hum of activity takes over.

Naturally, this is only to be expected at some time or other during the course of one's lease, particularly if it is a lengthy one, but, all the same, it comes as something of a shock. When this came about on my own shoot I knew full well that I should have to tolerate it for the next seven years, the time scheduled for the completion of the felling and thinning which was being undertaken.

Any form of keepering, except a few forays after vermin with the gun at weekends, was out of the question. I have long learnt the disadvantage of maintaining a network of tunnel-traps when gangs of workmen, many of them recuited casual labour, are on the place for five

83

days of the week. When forestry roads were built in my woods, some years ago, I lost, on average, one humane trap per week. No matter how well there are camouflaged in specially made wooden tunnels, a countryman, with some experience of vermin control, usually knows where to look for them. Apart from the inconvenience and the cost of replacing this equipment, the fact remains that the traps will not be doing their work if they are constantly being removed, or sometimes merely sprung, as happened on many occasions in my case, when a particular worker merely disliked the idea of traps, but had no desire actually to steal them. I was amazed at the interference which my hoppers underwent, considering that they were merely empty 5-gallon oil-drums with holes knocked in them.

So, weighing up the situation, with the prospect of a lean seven year spell before me, I decided that I would have to be content just to bide my time. I actually signed another lease, its termination coinciding with the completion of the forestry work. The question is, just what must I do, during this time, to ensure that the place is not entirely devoid of game when the time comes for me to rebuild.

Firstly, the rearing and releasing of pheasants is something which just is not practicable here. They would never stay within my boundaries with all the disturbance. Likewise, wild birds cannot be expected to breed either. Therefore, I must adopt a 'cocks only' policy during the shooting season, whenever I am fortunate enough to come across the odd pheasant or two. I shall feed my woods by means of straw bales broken up, and grain scattered amongst them. In this way, unless the man intent on interfering with my feeding-points goes to the trouble of raking it all up, and taking it away in sacks, there is little he can do to prevent the birds feeding.

The gun must play a prominent part in vermin control now, unassisted by either traps or crow-cages. It must be used more efficiently than ever before. Time must be spent in waiting for carrion crows once their nests have been located. The crow call and the decoys must be used to the full, and there is always the chance of accounting for a stoat or grey-squirrel whilst performing this duty.

Should a wild pheasant happen to nest in a quiter place on my shoot, then everything possible must be done to protect the sitting bird. I resort to such steps as encircling the spot with a wide ring of creosote—a trick practised by gamekeepers of the last generation, and scoffed at by the modern keeper. Effective or not, it is worth a try, anyway.

My flight-pond should not be affected too badly by the constant disturbance, for forestry workers and contractors are only too eager to head for home long before dusk. All should be peaceful by the time the mallard and teal decide to flight in. Of course, any duck which are in the habit of using my pool as a daytime rest will be prevented from doing so, but they soon change their routine to a nocturnal visit. I am a confirmed optimist. Indeed, I have to be, in order to survive the trials and annoyances which I know will beset me during the coming years in these hills.

Consequently, I have sampled gamekeeping as it was known by the older generation, in the days before the artificiality which exists on so many of the estates today. I would say, quite honestly, that it is much more interesting. One is not catering so much for the protection of semi-tame poults, which have no idea of how to combat the dangers of the wild, but rather assisting a natural process.

I was very pleased, indeed, to see a partridge on the edge of my woods, something which is comparatively rare in this type of hill country. Was its mate sitting on eggs? Once more I was optimistic. Then, on the very same day, I put up a woodcock on one of the woodland rides. There could be no doubt in my mind that it had stayed here for one purpose only—to hatch, and to raise its young in woodlands which it found to be acceptable, rather than to migrate.

I accept such a challenge not only with optimism, but with enthusiasm. There are no set rules. One must play the game from day to day, in an attempt to make something out of nothing, to conserve and to shoot at the same time.

There is one small crumb of consolation, though. Forestry work on any particular tract is seldom continuous. For months on end a shooting area is a hive of activity, and then, for no apparent reason, the contractors desert it for perhaps a year or more. A change in schedule, more pressing work, damage done by gales elsewhere to be cleared up, and a host of other reasons decided by those in administrative positions will give one a breathing space. It is nothing more than that. One never knows when the workers will return, tomorrow or next year? This uncertainty prevents a resumption of normal keepering duties. It is a time of waiting. A lull.

THE GAMEKEEPER AND ROUGH-SHOOTER'S DOG

As an amtateur keeper I rarely take my own dog round my shoot during the close season, particularly during April and May when there is a chance that he might stumble across a pheasant or partridge nest. If he did do so it would be out of sheer curiosity in the case of a hen bird which had laid her eggs too close to the main woodland rides. Nevertheless, the damage would be done, and a nest might be deserted for good. So I do not think that it is worth the risk.

The other reason why I leave my dog at home is because it is much harder to lecture a trespasser on the erring ways of his excited animal, which is tearing at random through the coverts when one's own dog is apparently in a position to do the same. I prefer, then, to set an example which I expect everybody else to follow.

With regard to the professional gamekeeper let us examine the requirements of his own particular dog, whether it be labrador, retriever, or spaniel. First and foremost it will be required for picking-up duties during the shooting season. In many cases this dog will only be asked to look for a bird after a drive when the visiting dogs have failed to find it. Probably it is a more experienced animal than those which have been chasing about vainly in search of a lost bird, but the host will no doubt want to give his guests every opportunity to use their own dogs, or those which have been specially brought along by handlers, concerned only with picking up, and taking no part in the actual shooting.

Very often, during the months of November and December when the days are short, the keeper will spend the entire day following a shoot, searching for lost birds. I have known occasions when twenty or thirty pheasants have been added to the previous day's bag by diligent searching on the part of the keeper and his dogs the next day. Often pheasants, apart from those which actually manage to evade the dogs during picking-up between drives, cross a line of guns, and escape apparently unscathed, only to drop some distance away, out of sight of guns and beaters. It is the duty of the keeper in charge to conduct a thorough search of the particular ground which has been shot over as soon as possible after first light the following morning.

Primarily this should be done with the humane aspect in mind, but naturally the tenant will want to gather every bird possible, rather than leave them for the vermin to clear up.

One vital use which a keeper will have for his dog on an estate

5-2 The Spaniel: a good rough-shooter's dog.　　(Photo: Lance Smith)

where pheasants are reared in large numbers is that of "driving in". After a morning feed, especially at feeding points where a pheasant is able to fill his crop in a remarkably short time, the natural tendency for this bird is to wander off. It has no fixed destination in mind, but behaves rather like its human counterpart who, after an exceptionally large and satisfying meal, decides to "walk it down". The danger here lies in the fact that the pheasants will wander on to a neighbouring estate where they may find the food more acceptable, and decide to stay, or else stray on to unkeepered land only to be shot unscrupulously. The only way in which the keeper can prevent this is by walking his fields with his dogs, towards his woods, and forcing every straying bird to fly back whence it has come. On many large estates this is a full-time job to be carried out daily, by one of the keepers, throughout the whole of the shooting season. Without a good dog this task would be impossible.

The keeper on many estates is responsible for keeping the local rabbit population in check. One may argue that this could be carried out satisfactorily by means of ferrets, snares, and gas. To some extent this is true, but remember that in many areas the habits of the coney have changed. It no longer uses warrens to the extent that it did prior to myxamatosis, thereby rendering the use of ferrets and gas not nearly so effective. If rabbits are occupying impenetrable cover then the use of these two major weapons will be nullified anyway. This only leaves snares. Effective as these may be if set by an experienced man, they require to be looked at twice daily, and this means time, time in which the keeper could be attending to more pressing duties. Jobs such as "driving-in" would be neglected, and the bag at the end of the season would be lessened considerably.

Therefore, the keeper must make use of his dogs, and organise a few back-end forays to keep the rabbit population in check. This can be a very pleasant interlude in the normal keepering routine, and most keepers enjoy a day or two spent in this fashion, mostly during the months of February and March. An invitation extended to the neighbouring keepers will usually result in a day or two spent on their estates, and a good time will be enjoyed by all, with a most necessary job of work being carried out at the same time. This method of shooting rabbits over dogs in rough cover can be very effective, and I have known some quite sizeable bags made in this way.

So it is evident that a good working gundog is *vital* to a keeper, but at the right time. During late spring and summer this dog will have to be content to remain in the kennels, apart from daily, regular exercise, but his day will come when the leaves begin to turn. Then he will be kept busy, and it is important that his health and fitness has been looked after during the months of confinement. Wily cock pheasants, unable to fly, that have evaded some of the best dogs in the area, will have to be found and despatched. Rabbits, relying on the protection of thick gorse bushes and acres of rhododendrons, will have to be bolted to the waiting guns, and dog and keeper must work as a team, each relying on the other to get the job done.

So it is with the roughshooter. His dog must be of similar quality, a hard worker, capable of finding, flushing, and retrieving birds. There is no need for 'field-trial' standards. Yet the hill-shooter's dog requires even greater stamina. His work will be the hardest of all, and it must be borne in mind that for every mile covered by its master, the dog will double or treble this.

I once had such an ideal dog. I doubt if I shall ever find a better friend or worker. Sadly, and coincidentally, he passed away in his fifteenth year on the very same night when that freak gale destroyed 'Buzzard Wood', related earlier in this book.

FEMALE GAMEKEEPERS

In these days of equality of sexes it is only to be expected that at some time the fairer sex will answer the call of gamekeeping. Indeed, I have known of at least one lady gamekeeper for some time now.

I first saw the article in one of our Sunday newspapers concerning what the writer termed as "the only lady-gamekeeper in the country". As I read it, I suddenly realised that I was only too familiar with the situation, for the estate in question was less than two miles from my own shoot. I have never actually met the lady herself, although I knew her father, the gamekeeper, quite well. How the national press obtained the basic information I do not know, although they are capable of infiltrating into the remotest of our rural areas and, alas, all to often they misinterpret what they see and hear. They had certainly found their way up into my area of the border hills.

The true facts behind this particular case stem from a serious illness which the keeper himself suffered some time ago. His daughter had always helped him in his work, so she was not entirely unfamiliar with the extra duties which fell to her when her father became incapacitated. All the same, one cannot help but admire her for taking on the task of rearing, and looking after, 1,000 pheasants, plus attending to an extensive round of tunnel-traps. However, the press seemed to regard her somewhat in the light of another 'Calamity Jane', stating that she "set forth, armed with a .410 shotgun, for the purpose of bowling over foxes and rabbits".

I know of many keepers who rely on their families to assist them, particularly at rearing time, and often wives and daughters are as knowledgeable in the problems which arise between hatching out and turning the poults into the woods, as are their husbands and fathers.

I must confess that I have never heard of a full-time lady game-keeper. There may be one somewhere, though, a dedicated woman who has so far escaped the publicity of the press. Logically, there is no reason why a female should not occupy the post of gamekeeper. Many of them take an ardent interest in shooting, some even carry a gun themselves, particularly on the grouse moors and driven pheasant beats. So, why should they not become keepers?

Often, a woman is able to handle broody hens, day-old chicks and poults, with more patience and care than that shown by a man. She already has the maternal instinct herself, and probably understands the worry and distress of a mother hen better than any man could possibly hope to do. Possibly the birds realise this, also, responding more readily to her sympathetic and encouraging tones. Likewise, tunnel-trapping, which, after all is only commensense, should offer no real problems, provided she is physically fit and able to walk several miles each day in order to inspect her traps.

The only real stumbling block in the path of a woman who decides to make a career of gamekeeping, is the necessity for heavy physical work at certain times of the year. Pheasant pens, for instance, require moving daily during the rearing season. A considerate shooting tenant would probably see that the pens were either lightweight, which could be moved easily to fresh grass, or otherwise he would provide her with a helper in the form of a trainee keeper, a boy to whom hard work was the accepted order of the day. This, of course, is the answer to the success of any female gamekeeper. Her skill and devotion would be supplemented by the work-rate of a strong, male assistant. He, also, would be able to safeguard her from poachers who sought to capitalise on the fact that the estate was guarded by a keeper who was not physically capable of meeting them on their own terms.

Perhaps, in these modern days when the sport of shooting requires technical knowledge, rather than the traditional breed of gamekeepers, who were the backbone of the estates in days gone by, we may see in the "situations wanted" columns, a lady advertising for a job.

THE LEGEND OF A GAMEKEEPER

I feel that this chapter on gamekeepers would be incomplete without a mention of the legend of 'Keeper's Kop', an almost forgotten story of a keeper who trod the same ground which I now walk, in the days prior to the Kaiser's War.

The half dozen or so stunted pine trees stand out, stark and twisted, on the summit of the small hillock. They are grotesque in shape, playing tricks with the mind if one studies them for long enough. The one on the side nearest to the road might resemble a bent and deformed ogre one day, an aura of evil thrown around it by the black storm clouds gathering behind it, whereas, on a bright summer morning, in full sunshine, that very same tree will conjure up a picture of a kindly old woman on her way to market, a basket of eggs on her arm. The ones which are grouped closely together, serving as a windbreak for this lone pine, might be wild animals, relics of the middle ages or Saxon times, or perhaps they are a group of merry-makers, returning from a country fair or the inn, on a balmy, summer evening. One sees the scene as the mood dictates.

It is a strange place this 'Kop', somehow resembling a 'dry land island', a clump of lush green rising out of a sea of ploughed fields and growing crops, set apart from the large fir plantations, an acre and a half of land which has defied progress and modern agriculture. Tenant farmers over the decades have accepted it for what it is, an unconquerable stronghold, impregnable, a forgotten wilderness in a land of intensive farming.

This place has known several names over the years. I have heard it called 'Mount Zion', 'Spion Kop', and, more commonly, 'Keeper's Kop'. The latter name appeals to me most, for I have heard the origin of it, whilst the others are merely borrowed from other sources. To me it will always be 'Keeper's Kop', for the story goes that a young apprentice gamekeeper, many years ago, used it as a meeting place whilst he

5-3 'Keeper's Kop': a legend lingers on.   (photo: Guy Smith)

courted the daughter of the wealthy landlord. It was an ideal spot, for it served as a vantage point over the surrounding flat countryside, and the lovers stood little chance of being surprised here—an unseen approach was virtually impossible. I choose to believe the tellers of this story for, were it untrue, it would surely have had a happy ending. The fact that it has not, convinces me of its validity. The secret romance was eventually discovered by the unfortunate girl's father and, as a result, she was sent away to London to live with relatives, whilst the gamekeeper was dismissed from his duties. However, long afterwards, when the girl had eventually forgotten her teenage love affair and married into a rich city family, the keeper would return to this grassy hillock, from a town some fifteen miles away where he had since found employment, and spend his leisure hours alone there with his memories. I do not know what was the final outcome of the whole business, for it all took place long before the Great War. Possibly his remains lie buried in foreign soil along with thousands of others who gave their lives selflessly.

As for 'Keeper's Kop', it is still the same today as it was then. Perhaps the trees are more stunted and twisted than before, but basically it is much the same, a forgotten oasis. It is one of the few places which are likely to stand the test of time, for nobody wants it, and nobody cares.

THE GAMEKEEPER'S DUTIES

Gamekeeping, whether amateur or professional, is not merely a matter of patrolling one's acreage with a gun and killing as much vermin as possible. As has been explained in a previous chapter the majority of predators are accounted for with traps, and success will only be obtained after a lot of hard work. Nevertheless, this alone is not sufficient. *Organisation* is the key to success, and it is hoped that the under-mentioned table of duties to be performed throughout the year will be of help to the amateur. However, this in itself is only a guide, and should be used only as a *basis* for keepering, for tasks vary from area to area. For instance, the moorland gamekeeper will not be concerned with the rearing of game. His task will be to control the vermin, burn the heather systematically in the spring so that the new shoots which provide the staple diet of grouse can grow in abundance, and to safeguard the nests of grouse and blackgame.

93

SPRING

With the commencement of the close season, those who catch up their surplus pheasants for laying must start right away. The birds must be penned in the ratio of one cock to six hens. Those who do not rear, owing to the nature of their particular shoot, still have plenty to do. Now is the time for a full-scale onslaught on vermin. Trapping equipment must be serviced, and a network of tunneltraps planned throughout the shoot as explained in Chapter 3. This will mean hours spent daily in inspecting these. The gun should be carried at all times because the opportunity of a shot at a carrion crow or other corvines must not be missed. These are apt to show up just when you least expect them.

This is the one time of the year when shooting will not do harm around the coverts, neither driving off birds which you are trying to hold within your boundaries in readiness for your next shoot, nor disturbing sitting hens. Take advantage of February and March. You could also arrange one or two pigeon shoots. During the 1950s organised Saturday afternoon pigeon battues were very popular throughout February and March, almost every gun turning out in an attempt to keep the birds moving from wood to wood. In latter years, though, the interest seems to have waned. Possibly the withdrawal of free or subsidised cartridges for this purpose by the Ministry of Agriculture has something to do with this. In any case the results left much to be desired, and a couple of experts could kill almost as many pigeons over decoys in one day as a whole county filled with casual shooters could possibly hope to do. Nevertheless, there is no reason why you should not invite a few friends and one or two of the local farmers along to try their hand at roost shooting. Even if the bag is small the sport will be appreciated by everybody, particularly those who have nowhere to shoot at all.

Once April arrives you must be on the lookout for pheasant nests in the wild. Do not disturb your woodlands too much looking for them, but if you happen to come across the odd one or two then take steps to safeguard the sitting bird. One or two fox snares can be set in the vicinity and you might catch Reynard in time, but most important of all you must be on the lookout for trespassers. It is the person with the unruly dog who will be your worst enemy. Although the Forestry Commission generally allow the public to walk in their woods they will not tolerate uncontrolled (i.e.; off the leash) dogs. The favourite excuse by those erring in this way is that 'my dog won't catch game'. It doesn't need to. Once a sitting pheasant is disturbed the damage is done.

SUMMER

By May the rearing programme should be in full swing and you will be kept busy feeding your birds and moving pens daily. In all likelihood the tunnel-traps will have to be withdrawn simply because you will not have the time to look at them. In any case, traps rarely catch well during summer, but it is a good idea to keep one or two in operation around your rearing field to catch the odd stoat, weasel, or grey squirrel which comes in search of easy prey.

May 12th has for years been the traditional opening day for rook-shooting. Like the organised pigeon battues, though, it seems to have lapsed in latter years. It is not a good time in which to have excessive shooting on your land, but the fact remains that the rooks must be thinned out, and this is by far the best time to do it just as the fledglings are about to leave the nests, perching on the branches without having attained their full powers of flight. If your land is well away from roads and bridle-paths it is worth applying to the police for a firearms certificate, and buying a rifle. This weapon is far quieter and much more sporting where rooks are concerned.

August will be a hectic month. Those who have reared their own pheasants will be busy taking them to the woods. Release Pens should have been built or existing ones renovated before now, and the wire netting must be checked to ensure that there are no holes by which birds can escape or foxes can enter. More vigilance than ever will be necessary now because with your pheasants confined in this way they will be helpless should poachers decide upon a raid.

Flight-ponds should be fed now in readiness for the start of duck-shooting on September 1st. You will need to observe how many duck are coming in to feed nightly in order to plan your first shoot. Often a late harvest coincides with the opening date, and then the birds will forsake your pool for easy pickings on the stubble fields. When this happens, unless of course they are stubbling on your land, shooting may be delayed for a fortnight or so.

AUTUMN

A few forays after partridge can be organised, but keep well clear of your woods where your pheasant poults will be spending most of their time. Partridges in the hills, however, are generally something of a rarity; so often the upland shooter will have to wait until October 1st before starting to shoot seriously.

With the fall of the leaf pheasant shooting begins in earnest. The duck will be back on the pools, and now is the time to enjoy the fruits of all your labours. Then, with the November moon the woodcock will arrive, and for the next few weeks you can forget your keepering and concentrate on shooting.

WINTER

You must be on the lookout for poachers during the month of December. Even in these modern times the lure of illegal game still seems to create an aura of romance with some people. Poaching is nothing less than stealing, and those who transgress between the hours of sunset and sunrise run the risk of being sent to prison if caught. So the night poacher will be far more desperate than the one who mooches through your woods on a Sunday morning. Always proceed with caution if you suspect that night-poaching is taking place. Where possible locate a vehicle which appears to belong to the poachers, take the registration number, and contact the police as soon as possible. All the pheasants you have ever bred are not worth getting yourself killed or seriously maimed for.

Really Christmas is both the highlight and the end of the shooting season. Most syndicates organise something rather special for the festive season, and then it is 'cocks only' up until February 1st. However, there is still plenty of sport to be had during the latter weeks. Now is the ideal time to ferret those warrens which you have had to ignore up until now due to more pressing duties. Hare drives can be organised, and if the weather is hard then there will be plenty of pigeon shooting.

Thus the season draws to a close; and then it is time to begin the keeper's year all over again in readiness for the next.

CHAPTER 6

Trespassers, Poachers and Sheep Rustlers

DISTURBANCE TO WILDLIFE

One is always inclined to associate remote hills with a permanent air of peace and tranquility. On a hot summer's day nothing seems to stir, except for the buzzard drifting lazily overhead in the deep blue sky, and the buzzing of bees collecting pollen is drowned only by the cooing of woodpigeons in the surrounding Forestry Commission plantations. In winter, when the landscape is covered by a carpet of snow, noise is conspicuous by its absence. The occasional car passing through the narrow lanes seems to be almost an intruder in this refuge from the march of civilisation and progress.

However, there are time when, legitimately or otherwise, this typically English countryside scene, becoming rarer every year, is reminded that it exists in the twentieth century, and is by no means invincible from the spread of modern customs and ideas.

During my first few weeks of the tenancy of my hill-shoot above Clun, I was convinced that nobody would set foot on my land between my regular visits, except perhaps for the odd forestry worker, going about his duties, or a shepherd in search of a lost sheep. So confident was I on this matter that I placed an intricate feeder, which I had spent hours in constructing, within full view of a main woodland ride. I made no attempt to conceal it, whatsoever, and on my return, about three days later, I was astounded to find that it had completely disappeared. After some time wasted in diligently searching the surrounding undergrowth, I located the missing hopper—at the bottom of a nearby woodland pool! What on earth, I asked myself, would anybody be doing up *here*? I have since repeated that question on innumerable occasions, for in a place which is so far removed from the urban areas, and well hidden by a maze of intricate lanes, somebody always seems to find their way there.

I am not averse to strangers, providing they behave themselves and do not exercise their dogs on my land off the leash, but it is infuriating to find that some item of keepering equipment has not only been discovered, but interfered with, by persons unknown. Even this beautiful border country is not exempt from the hooliganism which we have come to accept but not to condone, in more populated areas. The trouble is that these incidents are so isolated and unexpected, that they seem far worse than they did when they happened to me on previous shoots which I rented, nearer to the larger towns.

The worst disturbance my hillshoot ever underwent, occurred some four or five years ago. I arrived there one week end, and my first thoughts were that the whole place was under Motorway construction. Bulldozers were in evidence, trees were being felled, and the usual air of peacefulness had gone. My enquiries revealed that the Forestry Commission had decided to make a network of rough roads throughout the woodlands in preparation for the time when the trees would have to be felled, and also to assist the fire brigade to reach the necessary place should we be unfortunate enough to experience a forest fire. Fair enough, one would say, a reasonable enough explanation. Agreed, but my landlords had not thought to give me prior notice of their intentions, and I had released a batch of hand-reared pheasant poults only the previous week. These I never saw again, and any wild pheasants, which I might have been fortunate enough to have in my woodlands during the early part of the season, fled to a quieter place. The work went on for five months, beginning in September, and being more or less completed by the end of January, the duration of the shooting season. All forms of wildlife deserted me, and I have no doubt that my neighbours on all sides were delighted when the head of game on their land doubled overnight! It certainly was an unfortunate state of affairs, and it took almost twelve months for things to return to normal. However, this upheaval was unavoidable as this work had to be completed sometime during the next three years. My only grounds for complaint were that I knew nothing whatsoever about it, otherwise I should have turned my poults down on another side of the hill. Anyway, it was a necessary disturbance, and time has proved that the forestry roads have been a benefit to me. I can now transport game food to the required places, quite easily by vehicle, whereas before I had to carry it to its destination in smaller quantities. Most ills have their compensations.

During the summer months picnickers can present quite a problem to landowners and shooting tenants. I would hasten to stress that not all visitors to the hills at weekends are nuisances. Indeed, I have enjoyed a chat with many who have motored out and found my place, quite by chance, on a sunny Sunday afternoon. However, it always pays one to investigate a parked car, for negligence may lead to trouble later. Fire is the main danger where these people are concerned, and this is my main reason for paying such close attention to them. Many urban dwellers see no danger in their small spirit stoves. and are quite happy to boil their kettle behind a shelter of dead undergrowth. They become quite indignant when I point out to them the error of their ways. One accident could result in the loss of hundreds of thousands of pounds worth of growing timber, and, from my own point of view, years of game conservation would have gone to waste. I should be faced with the prospect of completely rebuilding my stock of game, using as a foundation acres of fire-devasted woodlands. A formidable and unenviable task, indeed.

Blaring transistor radios are a source of annoyance. I would like to be able to ask the various species of wildlife what their opinion is regarding this latter intrusion of privacy and peace! However, I do not need to do so, for the scattering of pigeons from the nearest clump of trees the moment that one of these is switched on, in a nearby parked car, provides me with my answer. Unfortunately there is no law to counter this problem in the wilds, as there is within the limits of a city where noise abatement receives greater attention.

Disturbances to the countryside will not diminish. They will only increase along with the growing population, and we must be thankful that such places as our border hills exist, where peace and quietness reigns for the greater part of the time.

THE IMPORTANCE OF CONSTANT VIGILANCE

Little do the majority of people realise the importance of those few who patrol and watch over much of our fast diminishing countryside at weekends and holiday times, throughout the summer months. Mainly this lack of recognition is due to the fact that these guardians are, for the most part, rarely seen by the picnicker and hiker, unless, of course, these latter transgress. He who lights a fire in an unwise place in order to brew his tea, or ventures into areas where trespassing is forbidden, is soon confronted by one of these men. He may be a gamekeeper, an employee of the Forestry Commission, a National Trust warden, or perhaps someone like myself who has a vested interest in a particular tract of land, and takes these duties upon himself, voluntarily, in an attempt to protect his own place from the threat of the encroaching tide of progress, and a rapidly increasing population. The rewards are purely in one's own estimation of a job well done, and the knowledge of wildlife, crops, and forestry protected from the vandalism which is so rife in this modern age. He who has constantly to reprimand others for their misconduct will never enjoy popularity, and this is something which one has to accept. Few people outside our rural areas appreciate what this job entails, and he who has been admonished for some form of misconduct may very well have been genuinely unaware that he was actually doing wrong at the time. The following is an account of one such patrol I made, and is a typical example of what one may encounter on a fine weekend, when the world and his wife have descended upon the countryside.

It was warm, and the flies swarmed round me as I left my parked vehicle, and entered the thickly wooded hillside. I carried my gun, as usual, not that I was particularly intending to use it, but one never knows when it may come in handy. I am responsible for keeping the rabbit population under control on this particular 600 acres of Forestry Commission land, and whenever the chance of shooting a coney arises, I take it. Likewise, vermin such as carrion crows, jays and magpies, might present me with an opportunity which otherwise would be wasted. My yellow labrador, Remus, panted at my heels, constantly snapping at the black clouds of flies. I had not brought him for any reason other than much needed exercise after a week of 'semi-urban' walks, and that companionship which only the true dog-owner appreciates. On a day such as this he would certainly have been more comfortable remaining in the cool of the house, but he would only have paced restlessly round the garden until my return, so I yielded to his pleas, and brought him along. I kept him on a leash, primarily as an example to any whom I might meet and have to reprimand for the behaviour of their particular dog.

Suddenly, a rabbit bolted out of a clump of heather, and my instinctive snap-shot bowled it over before it reached the protective belt of trees opposite. The loud report of my shot echoed throughout the surrounding hills, and I felt almost guilty at having shattered the perfect peace.

About a mile further on I came to my furthermost boundary, where a rough bridle path separates these woods from an adjoining privately owned estate. As I emerged from the thick coverts, I noticed a vehicle pulled off this track, and reversed through a convenient gateway into my own woodlands. Keeping beneath the trees, I approached it as stealthily as possible, for one never knows whom one may meet up with in these wild and desolate places. As I got closer I could see that it was a dormobile, and the occupants, a man and a woman, had obviously come prepared for a lengthy stay, judging by the impedimenta which was piled up in the adjacent clearing. A kettle steamed on a spirit-stove, and, indeed, I felt quite heartless at having to disturb such a peaceful scene. They were very understanding, which made my job all the easier in explaining to them that they could, under no circumstances, camp here. Ten minutes later they were reboiling their water in similar surroundings in my neighbour's woods. I suppose I had done this worthy man a disfavour.

During the course of the next couple of hours I came across a middle-aged couple enjoying a stroll in the heart of the woodlands. I saw nothing amiss at first, and would have been quite content to pass the time of day, and leave them to enjoy their walk, until a large dog, the species of which it was quite impossible to determine, suddenly emerged from a belt of Norwegian spruce, hot on the trail of a large hare, some five yards ahead of it, and disappeared into another one opposite. The couple seemed to find this amusing, and even when I had pointed out the damage which their Fido was likely to do to nesting game, they came up with that statement which I have heard countless times, that "our dog wouldn't kill anything. He only chases them!" However, on their admission that they did not possess a leash, I pulled a 3ft long piece of string out of my pocket, and insisted that they made use of this until they were clear of my boundaries. After some argument they complied with my wishes, and we continued on our separate ways. Nowadays I always carry a spare length of rope for this purpose.

Eventually I emerged out of the thick woodlands on to the heather and rough grass of one of the neighbouring hill-farms. This particular flockmaster likes me to keep an eye on his upper fields whenever I pass this way. Once I found a cast sheep which would otherwise have perished in a very short time, and on another occasion I was just in time to rescue a helpless lamb from the attention of crows.

101

On this occasion, as I walked over the brow of a small hillock, I surprised a carrion crow which was just able to glide off the branches of a solitary thorn bush before my charge of No. 5 shot ensured that this particular bird would ravage no more defenceless lambs, or search out game birds' nests. The crow, in my opinion, is the worse villain of all, for it flies slowly, has the sharpest of eyesight, and little escapes its searching scrutiny. It is quite merciless in its plunderings, and a shot such as this gives me the greatest possible satisfaction.

The sun was beginning to drop behind the jagged range of mountains on my left, as I stood there, on what seemed to me to be the roof of the world. Somewhere on the heather covered slopes below me, a cock pheasant shouted, and, far away, a raven honked its approval of this peaceful setting also. There was a haze over the distant pinnacles, and this was an almost sure sign of fine weather on the morrow. Far below, on the winding narrow roads, I saw several cars heading back towards the denser populated areas. It was time I was leaving too.

POACHING

Throughout the ages poaching has always had an aura of romance about it, a false image which has been immortalised in fiction by such characters as Robin Hood. Offenders escape with paltry fines, and all too often even the magistrates themselves are apt to view the whole affair with tongue in cheek. Yet, poaching is simply *stealing*—the theft of another man's game. With the advent of the motor vehicle the mode of poaching has changed. Escape after a raid on a preserve is easier and faster. The days of surreptitious snaring of rabbits and devious ways of taking game by the old local 'moocher' are gone.

In the hills poaching is much rarer than in lowland areas where there are well-stocked game preserves. Mostly the danger comes from cars crawling through the narrow lanes, usually early on Sunday mornings, a .22 rifle or .410 placed ready to shoot at any unsuspecting species of edible wildlife through the open window. There is no logic behind this type of poaching. The present cost of petrol will far outweigh the remuneration from any game shot, and as the majority of the targets will be sitting, anyway, there is nothing sporting about the whole procedure. One can only conclude that this is an inbuilt heritage from those whose forefathers were poachers in a less mechanised age, and they have to satisfy their urge in this way, a poor substitution which is criminal.

Whilst I stress that I have no wish to add to the myth of romantic poaching, I relate the following account of a hill poacher in the Highlands of Scotland in an attempt to illustrate the vast difference between poaching then and now.

A HILL POACHER OF OLDEN TIMES

Alexander Davidson was born at Deeside, near Crathie and Balmoral in 1792, and died in the hills of Glenbucket in 1843. Many may not even have heard of him, and to others he is merely a legend, a gigantic red-bearded fellow, shrouded in the mists of time as he prowled his domains, over one hundred and fifty years ago, in search of stag, salmon, or grouse, according to the time of year, moving stealthily, yet, at the same time, fearing no man.

'Sandy' Davidson., as he was more familiarly known, was a true Highlander in every sense of the word. Equally loved and hated amongst his kinsmen, his character is depicted according to he who tells the story, but all agree upon one point. He fully believed in the legitimacy of his calling, poaching because he felt it was his right. He would never touch a hand-reared game bird, or a tree from a planted forest, but claimed that the deer in the hills, the wild grouse and ptarmigan, and the natural forests, belonged to no one, and were his for the taking. Consequently, he was branded as a thief and poacher, and for the latter part of his life he was forced to keep out of the clutches of the law, living a carefree and lonely life in the hills.

Sandy became a marksman with a rifle at highland gatherings in his boyhood days. He accompanied his father to many of these sporting events, for the elder Davidson was a man of massive strength, and a champion at such events as tossing the caber. However, it was at one of these highland games that Davidson senior was the victim of a terrible accident whilst wielding the cudgel, received a cracked skull, and died on the same evening.

It was due to this unfortunate incident that Lord Kennedy at Falar, took pity upon young Sandy, and offered him employment as soon as he attained his fifteenth birthday. He had witnessed the young Scot's prowess with the rifle at shooting matches, and having been a great admirer of his late father, he decided to take him on as an apprentice gamekeeper on his estate, high up near the sources of the Tilt.

One might have thought that Sandy would have welcomed the opportunity of such a post, the chance to spend every day in the hills he loved, a gun under his arm, and a dog at his heels. However, it was not to be, for the one thing that he resented was discipline. He longed for his freedom, the chance to roam the areas that took his fancy, not merely where he was directed to go by the head gamekeeper. Consequently, he terminated his employment with Lord Kennedy, offering as his reason for this that he objected to being made to work on the Sabbath!

Sandy was barely sixteen when he embarked upon his new life, constantly on the wrong side of the law, and destined to become a legendary figure of the Highlands, to some extent another Rob Roy.

His new life of "freedom" began with a taste of whisky smuggling, an exciting life for a boy who had a yearning for adventure, trafficking the illicit liquor amongst the isolated highland townships. He was fairly successful in this venture, managed to avoid arrest, and accumulated some valuable capital into the bargain.

Alexander Davidson deserted the small highland townships and took to living entirely in the hills. Many of his former associates and friends never saw him again, for he was wont to frequent only lonely crofter's cottages. During the spring and summer months he spent his nights out in the open, the heather his bed in times of dry weather, and when it rained he sought the shelter of convenient caves. His winter nights were spent in the straw barns of those who afforded him the hand of friendship. He was accustomed to standing for hours, waist deep in an icy mountain torrent, in the hope of landing a salmon, or lying for long spells in a corrie, in snow and ice, on the offchance of a stag showing itself within shot. It was the life he loved above all else, and having sampled it to the full, he had no mind to return to a civilised existence.

His hunting grounds were more extensive than those of any wealthy laird in the highlands of Scotland. He knew no boundaries, and poached in Aberdeenshire, the Mearns, Angus, Perthshire, and Invernesshire. Mostly he shot just after daybreak, or shortly before dusk, the wildness of the terrain affording him a choice of escape routes in the event of any gamekeeper appearing on the scene. It was usually the case of a quick shot, more often than not a kill, and then away to the forests like some vagrant will-o'-the-wisp.

In his own way, Sandy Davidson was one of the finest sportsmen who ever stalked the deer forests and grouse moors of Scotland. He respected the various seasons with a degree of honour which one would hardly expect from a man in his chosen mode of life. He would have no more shot grouse on August 11th, than he would have killed one during the summer months. It is probably this self-imposed code of honour which earned him the respect, and in some cases, the friendship of the local gentry. He was an excellent dancer, and it was many a banquet that he attended, his identity possibly unknown to the other guests. His host was well aware that he would only poach the game which he required for his immediate needs, and neither grouse nor deer would be slaughtered indiscriminately.

There are many tales, mostly handed down through the generations of crofters, of Alexander Davidson's exploits. One relates how, on the glorious twelfth, he followed, and eventually joined up with, a large grouse shooting party. The guns and ghillies were numerous, most of them having arrived on the previous day from distant parts of the country, so it was no small wonder that a great many of them did not even know their fellow sportsmen. The poacher mingled with them somewhere on the outskirts as they set off across the moors.

He shot well that day, his ancient double-barrelled flintlock accounting for several brace of grouse, and the odd blackcock. He even insisted on carrying his own birds, much to the relief of the ghilly. Perhaps it was fortunate that the host himself was unable to attend the opening day, and it was the head keeper who complimented Davidson on his marksmanship.

As was only to be expected, towards the end of the last drive Sandy disappeared, as inconspicuously as he had arrived, striding off back to the forests, his laden bag on his back, and whistling a tune as he went. He had shot alongside the landed gentry, and had excelled himself in the process.

There was only one occasion on which the highlander allowed himself the luxury of shooting hand-reared game, and this was done purely out of revenge. It occurred soon after he had been wrongfully accused of poaching on the Invercauld Estate. The following full moon found him threading his way stealthily through the large fir coverts which surrounded the Factor's isolated house. Pheasants were roosting in clusters in the trees, showing up plainly in the bright moonlight. Firing and loading as fast as he could, he began knocking those birds out of the trees. Many took fright, and clattered away to safety at the sound of the reports, but others, uninitiated in the ways of man, merely stayed where they were, awaiting certain death. This was probably the most unsporting act of Davidson's life, but he gained supreme satisfaction from it when lamps were lit within the house, and yet no attempt was made to investigate the shooting. The Factor had no doubt concerning the identity of the poacher, but he feared to face his enemy alone, in the dead of night. Consequently, Sandy was left to shoot his way back to his forest hideout, dragging a heavy sack of pheasants behind him.

Anyone living the life which Sandy Davidson had chosen, would have needed to be supremely physically fit, and able to endure hardships beyond the comprehension of the ordinary person. Indeed, the highland poacher was blessed with these qualities, but, even to a man such as he, the continuous rigour of outdoor life, and primitive living, had to tell sometime.

Thus it was, that on the 24th August 1843, a wandering shepherd found him lying peacefully in the heather, his long-barrelled flintlock gun resting across his chest, and a look of contentment on his bearded face. A second look, however, confirmed the old flockmaster's suspicions. Alexander Davidson had died in the way he would have wished, out on his beloved grouse moors, beneath the open sky, with the warm sunshine playing on his rugged face. He had asked nothing more of life, and he had fulfilled his ambitions. He had been a true highlander, and, above all, had known the meaning of freedom.

There were many Sandy Davidsons throughout Great Britain, and far rather would I have such a character poaching my shoot than the car 'cowboys' touring the surrounding lanes. Alas, times have changed for the worse.

SHEEP RUSTLERS

However, we are faced with something much more menacing in the hills than poaching. Sheep rustling is more prevalent now than ever before. The financial rewards are much greater than those to be obtained from poaching game, and as a result the type of men involved in this activity are ruthless, and it is an unwise man who investigates suspicious circumstances on his own.

I have personally come up against the work of these criminals. For two years these gangs have operated in the area around my own shoot.

The hill farmers were losing sheep in small numbers, often the odd one or two which were sometimes not missed for several days. Then one day a remarkable discovery was made in a quarry bordering my forestry thickets. Dozens of polythene sacks containing sheepskins had been dumped there! The stench was obnoxious. Police investigations followed. Some of the brands on the skins were identified as those belonging to neighbouring farmers.

It was akin to a crime mystery novel. The gang had been systematically raiding all the local farms, stolen scores of sheep, and then returned to the scene of their nefarious activities to dispose of the skins! Was it a clumsy attempt by the rustlers to throw suspicion on the locals, or was it an act of blatant defiance? Most of the animals had been shot with a .22 rifle, no doubt in conjunction with a sound moderator.

And then, a few weeks later, one farmer discovered several sheep limping and bleeding from shotgun wounds. Another mystery. Was it the efforts of an entirely different gang, unskilled in the art of sheep rustling? I am rather inclined to treat it as a warning issued by desperate men, a display of violence intended to discourage any attempts at vigilante patrols by the farmers.

Those criminals operate under cover of darkness, and from the discarded skins it is clear that they know their business from killing to butchering. Somewhere in the organisation there has to be a man with slaughterhouse experience, and on the black market each carcase is realising something in the region of £15.00.

This increase in rustling is not confined simply to my own particular area. It is prevalent throughout Wales and Scotland, in remote areas where sheep graze close to the roads. Arrests and successful prosecutions appear in the press from time to time, yet there are many who escape the clutches of the law.

It is a comparatively new evil in these peaceful hills, and it is the duty of everyone, whether farmer, shooting tenant, hiker, or weekend visitor to report any suspicious incident, taking the registration number of vehicles which seem to be involved. Only by a concerted effort can these cowardly nocturnal butchers be prevented from carying on a vile trade. Like those who shoot deer in the headlights of poaching vehicles, many sheep will be maimed, and die a lingering death on some remote mountain slope.

The areas are too vast for the police to patrol systematically. It is up to us, every one of us who cares for the welfare of our beautiful hill country, its wildlife and its livestock, to make life as difficult as possible for these rustlers. A system of vigilante patrols is the only answer.

CHAPTER 7

Pheasants in the Hills

UPLAND GAME

Hills and uplands in general are not conducive to pheasants, whether hand-reared or wild birds. I am quite emphatic about this statement, and I am fully in a position to make it, for the whole of my shooting rights consists of land 1,000 feet above sea level, planted by the Forestry Commission with spruce and pine. To the layman, these woodlands may appear to be ideal for game, offering warmth and shelter, but let him take a look inside one of these thickets. Apart from the trees on the outer fringe, almost every one is "dead" from the base up to the top branches., which are the only ones to see sunlight. The ground beneath the trees is usually a carpet of dead pine needles, with little or no undergrowth, and does not present an inviting prospect to any wandering pheasant. Natural food is virtually unobtainable in these dark forests, and the birds will have to rely upon what they can glean from the fields on the surrounding hill farms. Usually this proves to be no more lucrative, for most of this land is only good for grazing sheep. Most farmers, however, plant a field of winter feed for their stock, such as rape or swedes, but this will only serve as effective food or cover for game birds for the early part of the winter. These farmers are apt to turn their sheep out to graze these as early as the beginning of November, and the shooting tenant who has relied on these fields as the basis for his pre-Christmas shoots may well be sorely disappointed.

I have reared and released pheasants in this type of terrain. On reference to my game register the scheme would not appear to have been a success, but I do not work purely on figures alone. When I first rented this place, I only saw one pheasant during the whole of the first season. However, I was not to be discouraged by this state of affairs, for I had rented the land with the intention of building up a shoot, and not taking on a ready made one.

The main essential when contemplating a long term policy such as this, is not to overshoot it in the early stages. The fact that one has released fifty pheasant poults in the summer does not mean that one has to try and record that number shot at the end of the following season. Indeed, it would be detrimental to the whole scheme, even if it were possible to kill all the birds put down. After years of hard work, trying to introduce pheasants into a totally unsuitable area, my satisfaction is gained entirely from the fact that there are always a *few* pheasants scattered over the whole of my acreage. I am satisfied with a sporting shot occasionally, and a bird for the table. It is not my intention to try and make sizeable bags.

Artificial feeding is a must where pheasants are concerned, particularly so in "hungry" hill country. If it is not possible to feed regularly by hand, then "hoppers" must be installed, again taking care in their siting. Forestry plantations are ideal for hoppers, the lack of under-growth enabling the birds to feed without fear of enemies lurking nearby, and the food being afforded protection from snow by the thick branches overhead. I use wheat, whenever possible, to feed my pheasants, as this is certainly their favourite, and I have had far better results with it than when I have used barley.

Feeding must not be regarded merely as an enticement for pheasants, a means of encouraging birds into a particular place where they can be easily shot, perhaps a neighbour's pheasants from over the boundary. The purpose of it is to attempt to hold game in an area where otherwise they would not be found. This, of course, applies to hill country such as mine, and not to the well-stocked preserves of the lowlands where pheasants are fed into particular woodlands prior to shooting days. I try not to shoot in the immediate vicinity of my hoppers, otherwise the birds will associate them with death rather than a means of livelihood.

Some years ago, I was congratulating myself on having a record number of pheasant poults on my shoot. During September there were ample to be seen on the stubble fields after a very early harvest, and I contemplated being able to shoot a few more than usual without endangering my "resident" stock. Suddenly, they disappeared overnight. I could not understand the reason for this, and dismissed any idea of having been visited by poachers, for they would not have been able to

110

7-1 Bringing in the Kill: a pheasant shot in rape on the boundary of Forestry Commission woods.

(photo: Guy Smith)

clear the lot on land such as mine. For the next ten weeks I hardly saw a pheasant at all. Then, a fortnight prior to Christmas, they were back, and I was able to provide a few for the table during the festive season. I pondered over this state of affairs for some time, and the only conclusion I reached, was that they had found a field of winter feed for stock more acceptable than my woodlands. They had probably discovered some kale or rape outside my boundary, and had remained there until the sheep had grazed it off, when they had decided to return home. I consider myself extremely fortunate that the farmer, whose land they had used, had not been a shooting man, or if he was, then a first-class conservationist.

I had some success recently in drawing my straying pheasants together by feeding wheat into a field of turnips. This was done primarily to provide some sport for a guest whom I contemplated inviting to join me in a day's shooting. Unfortunately, soon afterwards, the farmer turned his sheep into this field, and within a matter of a fortnight the whole of this excellent cover was laid bare. Otherwise, it would have proved a useful feeding ground up until the New Year.

Anyone who rents shooting in hill country cannot expect a large return for his labours or his money. He must be prepared to shoot sparingly, and be content with a few pheasants for his own table alone. Usually there are ample rabbits, pigeon, and vermin to provide all the shooting one wants, whilst attempting to build up, methodically, a small stock of game. I find this type of sport far more rewarding than the shooting of larger numbers of reared pheasants on keepered lowland shoots.

PARTRIDGES

Partridges are even rarer in hilly country than pheasants. This, I believe, is due more to the absence of suitable cover and food, than to the climate. As if to contradict this statement, one season I sprung a covey of at least twenty on the fringe of my Forestry Commission woods, just after the close of the shooting season. I cannot account for their presence there, but I should welcome their return.

Game, generally, are more at the mercy of vermin in land such as mine, where cover and food do not grow together, than they are in arable areas. Foxes are more prolific, and harder to control in dense conifer thickets, and their depredations are therefore much greater. It is

Plate 3

Top : Friends of the Gamekeeper
Bottom : Gamekeeper and Companions

heartbreaking to discover evidence of three or four poults having met their end at the jaws of Reynard, only a few days after release. In my case, a release-pen is not practical, for I have to travel seventy miles each way to my shoot, and daily supervision would be impossible. Pheasants in a place of confinement, with no regular supervision, would be a far greater risk than those just turned into the wild. On the whole, though, I have been reasonably successful with my efforts.

I remember one day, whilst grouse shooting in another area of hill country, a member of our party killed a cock pheasant which was flushed out of a patch of dense heather. A local shepherd, who was shooting with us, remarked that that was the first pheasant which he had seen there since the last war!

SHOOTING ON A MORE ORGANISED BASIS

November is virtually the middle month of the shooting season, yet it is only now that pheasant-shooting really begins in earnest. The harvest will have been reaped, even after a wet summer, and the trees will be bare, the dead leaves forming a thick golden carpet in the coverts. This is the time when the large bags will be shot on well-stocked estates, and the gamekeeper's worth will be seen by the number of birds which the beaters put over the guns.

The rough-shooter, also, must make the most of the next few weeks if he is to capitalise on all the hard work which he has put in during the summer months. The days will be drawing in now, especially after the clocks have been altered, and an early start is essential if the day's programme is to be completed without undue haste. Many syndicates enjoy a cooked meal at mid-day, usually prepared and served by the gamekeeper or farmer's wife, but I would be inclined to advocate a few sandwiches, washed down by a bottle of ale, and a full repast at the end of the day, if so desired. A full course luncheon will waste at least an hour of good shooting time, possibly more, as even the keenest of sportsmen are apt to linger over good food. Also, one is inclined to be less enthusiastic about walking long distances after a heavy meal. Reflexes, generally, will be slower, and many a pheasant, which would otherwise have been counted amongst the number of head shot when darkness closes in, will be chuckling gleefully up to roost, congratulating itself on yet another successful gauntlet run.

WOODCOCK—A BONUS

November is the month of the Woodcock, that will-o'-the-wisp of the woodlands, which causes even the most experienced shooting man's pulse to beat that trifle quicker. This long-beaked, magical bird will generally arrive in this country at the time of the November full moon. It is quite uncanny, for one day a particular woodland will be devoid of woodcock, and the next they may be found there in considerable numbers. They offer possibly the highest standard of marksmanship, as they twist and jink through the surrounding trees, causing frustration amongst the line of guns, and a dozen or so empty cartridge cases may not have so much as a feather to show in return for their expenditure.

Seldom are woodcock flushed in pairs, and this factor, coupled with their tantalising, erratic flight, caused Bols of Holland to offer a prize to any sportsman who achieves a "right and left" in the presence of two witnesses. Should one be fortunate enough to accomplish this difficult feat, then one will receive a badge from this firm, together with a bottle of apricot brandy. Subsequent repeats of this performance will result in a further engraving of the badge, and another bottle of liqueur.

The rural scene is unpredictable during the month of November. Late autumn sunshine on golden bracken, incessant pouring of rain, thick hill fog with visibility so reduced that proceedings may have to be abandoned, or even an early, possibly heavy, snowfall, may be expected. The gamekeeper, or shooting tenant, must prepare himself to adjust his scheduled programme at very short notice. Only in the interests of safety, such as inpenetrable fog, should he call off the shoot, for this is the height of the season, and full advantage must be taken of every available shooting day.

December should assume an equal amount of importance in the shooting man's diary as the month which has just passed, but, unfortunately, it does not. The festive season is closing in upon us, and it always leaves me with the feeling of another waning shooting season, with thoughts already turning to next year. The keeper will already be looking out his cages for catching up adult birds for stock, and anyone who shoots a hen pheasant after Christmas will certainly be frowned upon by his colleagues. Whilst one must try to become conservation-minded, one cannot help but regret the shortness of the game seasons. It is November before shooting really begins in earnest, and by mid-December the best days are over, leaving us with 'cocks-only' days and hare shoots.

However, most shoots manage a Boxing Day outing. In many cases these are organised more for the benefit of the younger generation who are just beginning to follow in their fathers' footsteps in the shooting field. These are not 'serious' days in the true sense of the word, the members of the syndicate often leaving their own guns at home, and obtaining far more pleasure from seeing their offsprings bring down a pheasant on the wing, than participating themselves. Safety is of prime importance, for these youngsters must be set a good example in the early stages of their sporting careers. The bags on these Christmas shoots will be small, due not only to novice shots, but also to the festivities which are still in progress. Often a late start will be made, terminating in an early finish on account of the parties and other Yuletide celebrations which clash with these fixtures. In some areas, shooting is cancelled for that particular day in order to allow the local hunt to ride through the fields and coverts, and those who would otherwise have been shooting will often content themselves in the role of a spectator, and follow the hounds. Naturally, a light sprinkling of snow will add to the atmosphere of such a day.

Christmastime is not such a holiday for the professional gamekeeper as one would imagine. In fact, it is no holiday at all. During the weeks beforehand he must be on duty almost twenty-four hours per day, if he is to outwit the poachers, and the thieves who seek to steal Christmas trees and holly from his coverts. Night-watching will be called for, and the single-handed man will be expected to cope with this as well as his routine duties. Often, in this case, he will reduce his daytime work merely to feeding his woods, snatch a few hours daytime slumber, and then spend an uncomfortable night in a hut close to where the majority of his pheasants roost. Often such nocturnal vigils are nothing but a waste of time, and Christmas finally arrives without there having been a sign of either poachers or thieves.

The gamekeeper's family have to accept the fact that Boxing Day will be a normal working day for him. Perhaps his wife will also be engaged on cooking meals for the shooting party, depending, of course, on whether or not these latter are in any hurry to depart after the last drive is over in order to join their own families. There will be no "time off in lieu" for the man who has made the shooting possible, but possibly a few generous tips from the guns might help to make this holiday work

115

more bearable.

Likewise, the rough-shooter who has enlisted the help of a few young voluntary beaters should see that they do not go unrewarded.

THE SEASON DRAWS TO A CLOSE

January heralds the end of yet another shooting season. It is an unpredictable month regarding the weather, and a severe freeze-up, or a lengthy heavy snowfall, can virtually eliminate it from appearing in the game book at all. On the other hand, it may well be mild and sunny, with the promise of spring just around the corner.

The wise shooting man will shoot no hen pheasants, whatsoever, whether he is a gun in an organised syndicate or merely rents a small acreage of his own. These hens will lay the eggs which will form the basis of the following season's stock of game, and each bird shot now will mean a possible loss of a further brood of pheasants.

However, with regard to cocks, the more that are shot the better, and a ratio of one cock to six hens is an ideal situation if it can be achieved. A glut of cocks on a shoot after the end of the season is as detrimental as an abundance of vermin, and, should shooting be curtailed for any reason, such as hard weather, or an outbreak of foot-and-mouth disease, then one will be well advised to thin out surplus cocks, preferably by using a .22 rifle at the feeding points. This can be achieved without undue disturbance to the rest of the birds, and the proceeds from the game-dealer will be useful towards the upkeep of the shoot in general.

Possibly some of the best duck shooting of the season will be enjoyed during January, particularly during a spell of hard weather. Should there be a river running through the land in question, then the duck will be forced to use this once the flight-ponds are frozen. Sport can be at its finest now, but one must be prepared to cease shooting if the freeze-up continues over a long period, for the birds will become thin and starved, their edible and sporting qualities becoming considerably reduced. The winter of 1962/63 was a classic example of this state of affairs.

I try to dispel that depressing feeling that it is all over for yet another season. If I really feel like enjoying some good shooting at this time of year, then there are ample pigeons on the move, mostly winter visitors from the continent, rabbits to ferret, providing there has been no recent outbreak of myxomatosis, and always plenty of vermin in the form of jays, magpies, crows, and grey squirrels. Mostly, however, I leave these until the next month, concentrating my efforts, during the remaining few days, on attempting to find a wily old cock pheasant in the hedgerows.

All too soon, January 31st arrives. Pheasants can legally be shot on February 1st, but what is there in a day? It is now time to start all over again, and although I lose no time in preparing for next season, I have no wish to dismiss completely the one which has just closed. Valuable experience will have been gained, and one will be that much wiser when the following September arrives. Then the cycle will begin again.

OVER-SHOOTING

However, I cannot stress too strongly the disadvantages of over-shooting on any acreage, whether on upland or lowland terrain.

Throughout the whole of the British Isles there are hundreds of shoots which are grossly overshot each season, and the tenants and owners of these places are constantly bemoaning a poor season, blaming the weather, and finding a score of other excuses for the lack of game on their land. They are quite ignorant, or wish to remain so, of the true reason for their barren fields and coverts.

When talking of over-shooting, I am concerned mainly with the rough-shooter, and the semi-organised syndicates which do not employ a full-time keeper.

It is the rough-shooter who is the main culprit in most cases, and is detrimental to his own sport, as well as that of his neighbours. It is the duty of every shooting man to make some attempt to replace the head of game which he kills annually, by some form of conservation, the most important of which is the rearing and releasing of a few pheasants, partridge, or wild duck, according to which species his land is most suited. Naturally, the man who has no water on his land has no incentive to rear duck, and he who rents the shooting over grazing land with no cover whatsoever, would have no hope of holding any pheasants. In this case, very little will be taken out of the wild stock anyway, so this man can be excused a "no-rearing" policy.

I shoot my place regularly, and possibly to anyone who did not know my particular acreage, I should be the first to be accused of over-shooting when it was known that I was round with the dog and gun at

117

least once, and sometimes twice, each week. I would stress, however, that overshooting is determined by the *nature* of the terrain, and not the *size*.

A shoot consisting of three hundred acres or less, with woods that can easily be beaten through, and small patches of cover, cannot stand shooting on an organised, or semi-organised, basis more than once a fortnight. The fact that almost every yard of the ground can be covered by dogs, beaters, and guns means that virtually every head of game will be disturbed, and if harrassed to any great extent then they will seek quieter pastures. However, a ramble round the hedgerows in search of the odd cock pheasant, by a minimum of one or two guns, will not create undue disturbance, and a weekly foray of this nature will do no harm.

To return to the problem of my own hill shoot. This land consists of woodlands and forestry plantations of such impenetrable thickness that a party of five or six guns, aided by dogs, could spend a whole day beating it out, and still fail to flush a large proportion of the game there.

However, I adopt a method of shooting one half of the acreage on one weekend, and the remainder the following week. This ensures against too much disturbance, and, over the years, I have never had cause to worry over visiting the shoot too frequently.

A REGAL PHEASANT

I feel that this chapter on pheasants would be incomplete without an account of 'Blackie', a hand-reared melanistic mutant pheasant which originated on a commercial game farm, and eventually became a regal bird in his own right on my shoot. He was, indeed, a bird with exceptional characteristics.

Blackie, the melanistic mutant cock pheasant, first saw the light of day, or rather the artificial rays thrown by an electric brooder, in the battery-like confinement of a game farm in the south of England. His first few days were spent milling around with his hundreds of brothers and sisters, the strong trampling the weak, and every so often the gnarled, impersonal hand of a gamekeeper would reach in to remove the casualties. Life went on, day after day, in this monotonous vein, for there was no night, yet somewhere in these tiny fluffy balls of constant activity was inbred the instinct to survive.

When Blackie was almost a fortnight old, he found himself, with a

118

dozen or so other chicks, transferred to an open wire pen. The sunlight was so much more pleasant than the dim orange glow which he had known before, and he could amuse himself with a day long hunt for a variety of insects amongst the blades of grass. The pen was moved to a fresh piece of ground every day, so he never exterminated the ant population in his allocated area. As dusk fell, each evening, that same weather-beaten hand appeared through an opening overhead, and herded them, chirping and complaining, into the dark recesses of a warm coop. The hay on the wooden floor was soft and inviting as they huddled together in the unaccustomed darkness, sleep finally overtaking them. Fear was unknown to them, and once, when a prowling fox chanced to scratch at the outer boards of their shelter, they barely cheeped, presuming it was their guardian, who fed and watered them, and moved their enclosure to fresh pastures.

Blackie grew in size daily, surpassing even the other dozen or so poults with whom he was housed. Soon, that small pen became too crowded for them, and they were transferred to a much larger one with a hundred or so other pheasants. The mesh sides seemed to reach up and touch the cloudless blue sky above, and small trees and bushes grew inside. Some strange instinct prompted the birds to fly up into the branches of these to roost each night. The gamekeeper visited them, morning and evening, entering through a door in this massive pen, always taking care to lock it behind him before scattering the grain from his buckets amongst the undergrowth. He made strange noises as he did this, a tuneless whistle which meant one thing to the poults—food! Man was their protector, and they showed not the slightest fear of him as they pecked away beneath his feet, determined to devour as much of the corn as possible in the shortest time.

Six weeks later Blackie was showing signs of becoming a magnificent specimen of his strain. His plumage had a jet black sheen as he strutted with the arrogance of a dictator, brooking interference from none, and only too ready to do battle with any of the other cocks in his bid for supremacy. During a bout of pernicious feather-pecking amongst the birds, Blackie was one of the few who remained unscathed, yet everlastingly sought to dig his sharp beak into the feathers of one of his comrades.

Blackie developed a wariness, almost a hatred, of mankind on the day the old gamekeeper de-beaked him. His faith in his guardian was completely destroyed when he suddenly found himself helpless in those strong, brown hands. Struggle as he might, he was unable to avoid that sharp metal instrument which painlessly removed the lower portion of his beak in about a second, thereby destroying his ability to torment his brethren. His authority had been usurped. He was just another pheasant, a nonentity in a kingdom which he had once ruled.

Fate decreed that Blackie and I were to have a long-lasting association, and that he was to become king again. Shortly before this melanistic chick had begun chipping away at the shell of the egg which imprisoned him, I had signed a lease on my 600 acres of Forestry Commission shooting rights. This area was situated in wild, hilly country, and was almost devoid of game, being a stronghold for foxes, and other vermin. Unfortunately, my agreement was late in completion, and I had no time in which to hatch a few pheasants for the forthcoming shooting season. Consequently, I decided to invest five pounds in a cock and three hen pheasants, which I hoped would be the forerunners of the moderate stock of game which I would try to build up. Provided that they survived the perils of the wild, and did not stray, there was every chance that they would hatch two or three early broods the following season. I would take care to shoot no pheasants during the following year.

Thus, due mainly to my optimism, Blackie and three of his lady friends arrived at my local railway station, in a large wicker basket, one Friday night in early August. Their 150 mile journey had not gone according to schedule, for the carelessness of some porter had caused them to miss their connection at Euston, and, consequently, I finally took charge of them at midnight, after a frustrating four hour delay during which I had restlessly paced the platform of the station.

However, they appeared to be little the worse for their prolonged journey, and I consoled myself that I should be releasing them into the freedom of their new home as soon as possible the next day. In the meantime, they would have to spend the night, still in their container, in the garage.

I arose shortly after daybreak the following morning, and a peep through the inspection slats of the pheasant-basket reassured me that my charges were still all right. However, before I took them on the last lap of their journey, a 70-mile car ride to my recently acquired shoot, they would have to be ringed, for identification purposes, a task which I

120

certainly did not relish. Yet, it had to be done, so, after a hasty breakfast, I shut myself in the garage, and, opening the lid of the basket just enough to allow me to insert my hand, I quickly grabbed the first bird, one of the hens. Easy! A couple of seconds later, and she was back with her companions, a bright yellow ring securely encircling her left leg. The other two were no more difficult, and now only Blackie remained. I noted the evil sparkle in his eyes, as he regarded me from the further-most corner where he crouched. Perhaps, though, with such a fine, distinctive looking bird, a ring was unnecessary. I should recognise him anywhere. A number of excuses began flooding into my mind, and then, thrusting them aside, I plucked up courage, and my quick grab secured a firm grip on Blackie. He fluttered and fought, but the ring went on. I smiled to myself, but only for a second, for just as I was in the process of putting him back, he somehow managed to twist his neck round, and sink his beak into the fleshy part of my free hand. As I shouted in agony, I automatically released my hold on him, and next second a threshing wing caught me full in the face. Blackie made his bid for freedom. Like a black arrow he sped for the most likely looking exit—the garage window! The thud of impact was followed by a splinter-ing and crashing of glass, and then he was gone. Oblivious of the blood which was dripping from my left hand, I flung open the door, and dashed outside. I stood aghast at the scene which greeted me. Broken glass littered the concrete drive immediately below the window frame, and there, amidst the splinters, lay Blackie, a bundle of feathers blowing in the wind.

That which followed must surely rate as one of the most remarkable escapes in bird-life of all times. As I picked Blackie up, fully prepared to deposit him in the dustbin, he twitched, raised his head, fluttered, and tried to stab me once more. There was not a cut or an abrasion on his whole body, and all that he had suffered was temporary concussion following his collision with the window pane! I was greatly relieved when he was once more restored to the confines of the basket.

Some three hours later, after a two-hour journey by car, and a walk of some half a mile across rugged terrain, with the pheasant basket on my shoulder, I arrived at my destination, a grassy bank on the edge of a thickly wooded slope, overlooking the narrow winding road up which I had motored. My four pheasants were on the verge of the first freedom which they had ever known.

I opened the flap of the basket, and stood back. For some time nothing moved, and then, every so often, a small head would look outside, stare in amazement at the wide world of Nature, and withdraw. Thus it continued for the next half hour, until finally one of the hen pheasants stepped out on to the grass, and began pecking at some of the grain which I had scattered on the ground. Soon it was joined by another, and, after a space of a quarter of an hour or so, the third bird emerged. Only Blackie remained.

Finally, Blackie accepted the offer of freedom. Not for him the timid exit from his prison. Instead, he stalked out, proud and arrogant, gave me a look almost of contempt, and then performed yet another reamrkable feat. Although he had only so far used his wings to assist him in going up to roost in the game-farm enclosures, they obviously had strength far in excess of the majority of pheasants which are hand-reared under such conditions. He stretched himself, flapped his black wings two or three times, and then, suddenly, he was airborne, gliding almost effortlessly down the slope below, until, finally, he made a 'crash-landing' on a hawthorn hedge, some three hundred yards away. He perched there for a time, perhaps himself surprised at his achievement, until, with another effort, he fluttered down into a clump of bracken, and was lost to sight.

I remained watching the hen poults for a couple of hours or so, until, at last, they too, wandered off into the bracken. As I left for home, I had misgivings about the wisdom of my experiment. Had I not merely wasted my time and trouble, but also sentenced four young pheasants to death? When darkness fell, the hill-foxes would be on the prowl, seeking a hen or a duck which had escaped the farmer's notice when he shut up his poultry. What chance would four helpless pheasant poults, accustomed only to an artificial, sheltered life, have?

Yet, the following week, when I visited my land, I caught sight of the three hen pheasant poults foraging for insects on that same slope, but of Blackie there was no sign. Had this regal, fearless leader been the only one of them to fall prey to Reynard?

It was two months before I saw Blackie again, and when I did, the circumstances of his re-appearance caused me once more to marvel at the unconventional traits of this hand-reared melanistic mutant. Fully two miles from my shoot there is a small sleepy village, consisting of a few black and white timbered houses, a well-maintained Norman church, and a stream which flows alongside the one and only street. It was on the banks of this stream that I saw Blackie, as I motored by, his wicked, gleaming eyes seeming almost to recognise my car! The ring was still on his leg, and he was by now a much more mature cock pheasant. I pulled up, and sat watching him for some time, but he remained as immobile as the church tower behind him. He was still there when I drove away, and I told myself that I should never again find him within the boundaries of my shoot. He had obviously shown a preference for the lowland areas.

The week following Christmas brought a change in the hitherto mild weather. The hills were in the grip of a hard frost, and as I approached the woodland pool, covered by an inch or so of ice, I noticed the pheasant tracks in the light covering of snow, leading towards the reed beds. Remus, my yellow labrador, had scented something, and, at a word from me, he plunged into this mass of frozen vegetation surrounding the small expanse of water. Seconds later, with that challenging, mocking cry of 'ka-ka-ka-ka-kup' Blackie burst into view, hurtling skywards as though jet-propelled. I stood and watched him soar his way to freedom once more over the tops of the Norwegian spruce trees. I felt exultant beyond words at the continued survival of this melanistic cavalier.

Then, Blackie disappeared again. Nowhere was he to be found in the ensuing weeks, and although I expected him to hurtle out of every bed of bracken or gorse which Remus worked through, there was no sign of him. Spring came, and it seemed as though he had now truly gone forever.

Sometimes I pay a social call upon the old gamekeeper on the neighbouring estate, welcoming the opportunity to learn from his lifetime of experience. Thus, one warm June afternoon, I accompanied him upon a tour of his rearing fields. We wandered between rows of symmetrically placed pens, where pheasant chicks and poults of all ages basked in the sunlight. High overhead, a buzzard soared effortlessly, only the wire netting keeping him from an easy meal. On we walked, back in the direction of the keeper's cottage, behind which stood the large mesh enclosures which housed the adult birds, caught up in his woods in the early spring, in order to provide him with sufficient eggs with which to hatch his stock of pheasants. However, the laying season was almost over now, and shortly these birds would be turned back into the wild where some would even manage to rear a late brood.

Suddenly, I stopped in my tracks, staring into the pen we were passing at that moment. There, perched on a dead fir branch, his jet black plumage as immaculate as ever, and the yellow ring still proof of his identity, was Blackie himself. He met my gaze, and I would like to think that he knew me.

"You seem interested in that old melanistic," the gamekeeper had noticed my sudden interest. "Caught 'im up in one o' the cages in February. Can't figure out the ring, though. Must be a hand-reared bird."

I then proceeded to tell him the history of my roving melanistic mutant pheasant.

"You're welcome to 'im," he replied after he had listened to my story. "I'll catch 'im, and you can take 'im with you now, if you like."

I shook my head.

"No," I smiled, "release him back into your woods with the other birds. If he wants to come back to me, he'll come. Make no mistake about that!"

Blackie, it seemed, preferred my neighbour's land to mine. After his release, he resigned himself to a life of comparative ease in the region of Hurst Wood. Autumn came, and with the falling of the leaf, I feared for Blackie's life, for now pheasant shooting would begin in earnest, and the syndicate guns would look upon the melanistic as just another pheasant, purely a target for their guns.

The season progressed, but, judging by reports received from my gamekeeper friend, Blackie was leading a charmed life. Twice he had run the gauntlet of the line of guns, surviving both barrels from the best shot in that particular syndicate. Then, as though having learned from his experiences, he had been seen in the sanctuary of the keeper's garden on shooting days, pecking unconcernedly at a patch of dying sunflowers, whilst his brethren were being flushed by the dogs and beaters.

At last Spring came round again, and then, one day in late March, I caught sight of my wandering melanistic mutant on the edge of one of my plantations. Blackie had returned, perhaps to rule the kingdom which he had vacated.

The sequel to Blackie's life story, which I had so far compiled from my own experiences of him, and those related to me by the ageing gamekeeper, came from a retired schoolmaster who lived in a remote cottage bordering my shoot. It seems that this man spent much of his time sitting in his large bow window, and taking a keen interest in the wildlife around him. He studied the raven and the buzzard, and delighted in catching odd glimpses of Reynard on his prowls around the adjoining woodlands. However, one morning in early April, he was sitting surveying the surrounding rural scene through his powerful binoculars, when a sudden movement in the long grass in the field behind his house caught his eye. He focused his lenses more keenly, but for a time all he could see was the threshing of the undergrowth. Then, an amazing scene was revealed to him as, out into the open rolled two cock pheasants, locked in a struggle from which only one of them would emerge alive. One of the contestants, or course, was Blackie, whilst his opponent was a magnificently plumaged 'Old English' pheasant, the white ring around his neck already stained with blood. At last the monarch had been opposed, the champion challenged, and the royal battle could only have one ending. Blackie was ageing now, and, in spite of his tenacity, he was no match for the slashing beak and spurs of his younger adversary. Twice he was sent flying, and on both occasions he hurtled back into the fray, lacking none of his former ferocity, half his plumage missing, and his vision obscured by a steady stream of blood which flowed from a cut above one of those beady black eyes. Yet again he was felled, and this time he did not rise. A new leader had risen, but Blackie would not be forgotten.

His strain still lives on today. Every so often I come across a pheasant which has a distinctly darker shade in its plumage. Often it is wilier, more elusive than its conventional counterpart. When this happens, I know that Blackie is not dead.

NOTES ON PHEASANT REARING

It is unlikely that many hill-shooters will be rearing pheasants on a large scale. Upland territory does not appeal to this regal bird, and all too often they will stray to the valleys below in search of warmer climates and arable land. The barren woodlands and grazing fields have little to offer them. Hoever, it is always worth experimenting to see if your shoot will hold the odd pheasant or two.

In *Gamekeeping and Shooting for Amateurs* pheasant-rearing on the lawn was described in detail. In effect this entailed the buying of twenty day-old chicks and a broody hen, and attempting to raise a full brood on the limited space at one's disposal, rather than buying eggs and rearing

125

only a 60% hatch on the same ground. Overall, the former method is more economical. You still have the same amount of work to do.

A good broody hen is one that immediately squats on the ground when you put it down. The one which runs around clucking is no good, and will in all likelihood either trample or peck the chicks. These should be introduced to her gently *under cover of darkness*, and you must be patient. She will be uneasy at first, and if she pecks at them take them away at once. She may even mistake them for mice. It is always as well to have a second broody in readiness in case of accidents.

Should you decide to rely upon an artificial incubator then test it first to ensure that it maintains a steady temperature. Some, particularly those heated by an oil lamp, are inclined to fluctuate according to atmospheric temperatures.

An early start is essential if you are to raise two broods. Beginning in early May, and allowing for the pen being moved three times per week, this involves eighteen moves in all until the pheasant poults are ready for release. This takes us up to the first week in July, and as the first lot of poults are taken to the woods another batch of day-olds are introduced to the same pen on a fresh stretch of grass. The second phase of the programme should be completed by mid-August.

Whilst the full-time gamekeeper does not have the problem of space to contend with, the amateur can certainly give individual attention to his charges. The loss of one to him represents perhaps fifty casualties to his professional counterpart.

FEATHER-PECKING

Feather-pecking is the curse of all pheasant-rearers as the birds grow. It is caused by boredom, and whilst there is no certain cure for this then there are ways in which it can be cut to an absolute minimum. Mirrors placed around the inside of the pen will often amuse the poults for hours as they stare at their own reflections. Similarly, a lettuce suspended on a string from the roof of the pen will occupy their time. The best method is probably to de-beak the birds, using a strong pair of scissors, but unless one is experienced in this then unnecessary cruelty can be caused. Really it is a last resort.

OPEN-RELEASE

The Release Pen presents problems as has been explained in an

126

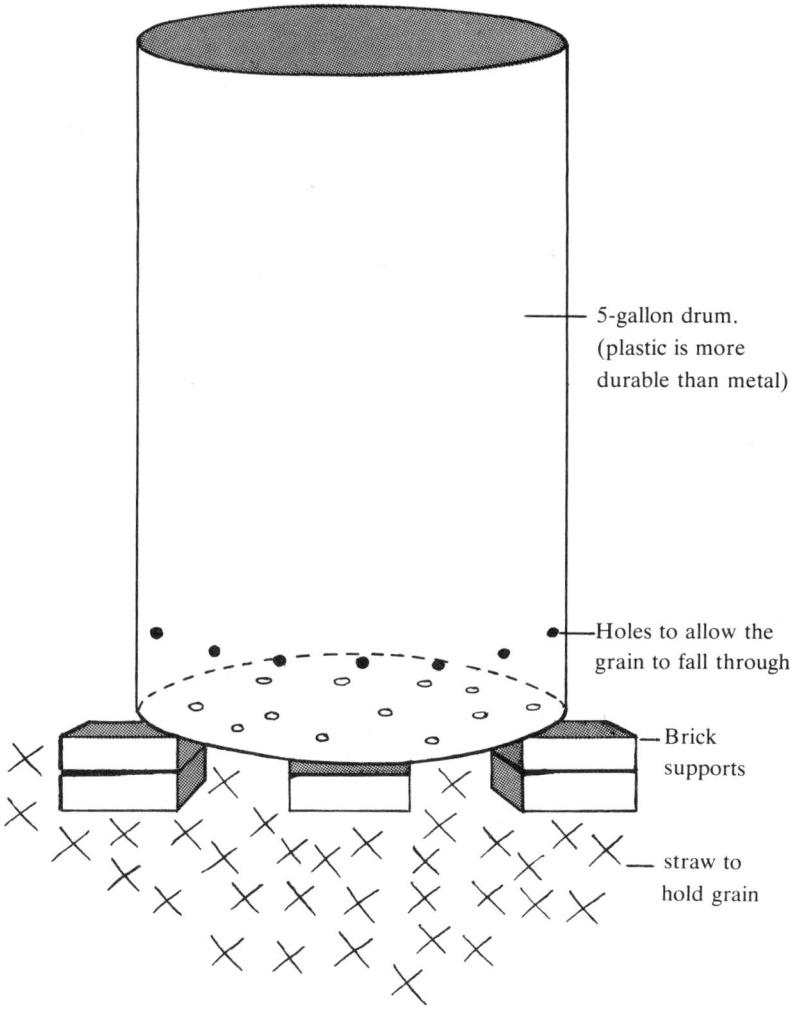

5-gallon drum.
(plastic is more
durable than metal)

Holes to allow the
grain to fall through

Brick
supports

straw to
hold grain

7-2 A Simple 'Hopper'. As the pheasants feed further grain will
spill out through the holes.

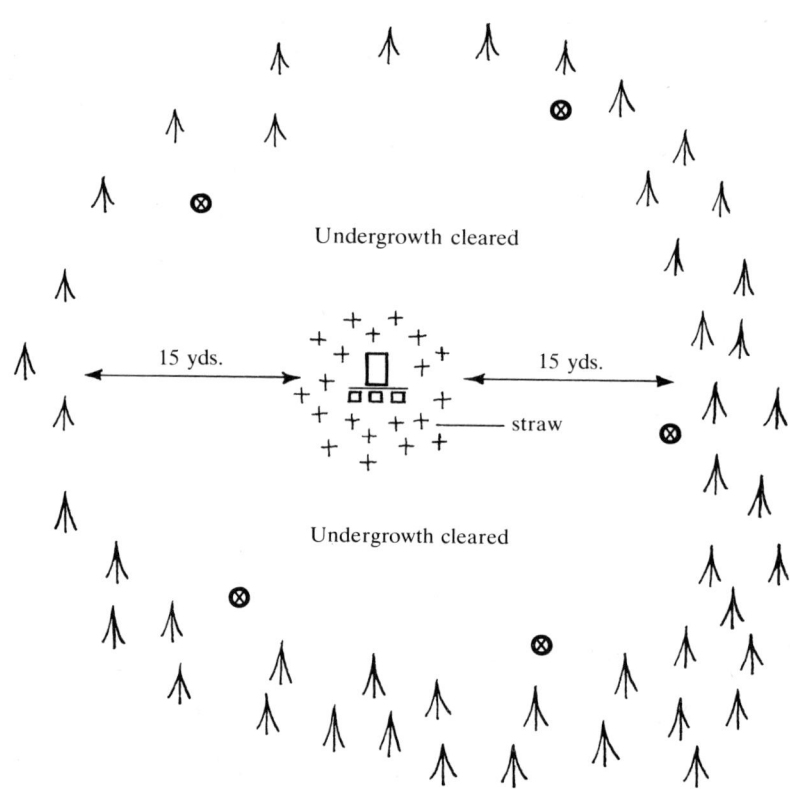

Undergrowth cleared

15 yds.   15 yds.

—— straw

Undergrowth cleared

⊗ = tunnel traps. Grain will always attract ground vermin.
Undergrowth which could hide a lurking fox should be cleared.

7-3   A 'Hopper' Site in thick woodland.

earlier chapter. Unless it is secure and under constant surveillance, then poachers and foxes will take their toll. This leaves us with only one alternative—to release the poults straight into the wild.

Branches placed in the pen, during those weeks when the pheasants are on the lawn, will give them some idea of what roosting is all about, something which is vital if they are to keep out of the clutches of prowling foxes during the hours of darkness. Where open-release is to be practised then the birds should be freed in the immediate vicinity of a farm. Often they will integrate with farmyard poultry for a time, and the author has even had experience of them going to roost in a hen-house along with the fowls!

Perhaps the farmer can be persuaded to feed them for you, and if their foster-mother is released along with them she will at least be able to offer them some protection by keeping them close to her around the farm. However, as the poults grow they will yearn for their freedom, but by this time they should be capable of fending for themselves.

A QUESTION OF SPECIES

Everybody has their own idea about which species to rear. The Melanistic Mutant seems to have the least inclination of all to wander, but, on the other hand, does not seem fond of high altitudes. Most game farms supply a mixture of Old English or Ring-necks unless other breeds are specified, and these are probably as good as any. It is helpful in tracing the movements of your pheasants if you include one or two Chinese each season. Their light plumage shows up easily, and they are recognisable at a distance. You will thus be able to determine whether or not your birds are wandering over your boundaries.

FEEDING

As mentioned already in this book, feeding is vital if you are to have any hope whatsoever of holding your birds. Daily feeding ensures that the grain does not become stale or mouldy, and also that it is not lying around the woods in quantity so that the pheasants, having eaten their fill soon after daylight, wander off. Woodpigeons may devour the majority of it, or you could invite an unwanted plague of rats or grey squirrels.

However, if you simply cannot feed your woods daily then the only alternative is a 'hopper'. The following illustrations 7-2 and 7-3 are a guide to simple construction and siting.

CHAPTER 8

Ducks and Woodcock

FLIGHT PONDS IN THE FORESTS

One does not associate hill country with wild duck. All too often, unless· there is an expanse of water such as a large reservoir in the vicinity, these birds have no reason to flight at such altitudes. Yet, the ubiquitous mallard, and sometimes the teal, are likely to turn up on any pond, however small 'and far removed from their normal flight lines. The frequency of their visits depends upon oneself. If you have water on your hill-shoot then there is no reason why you should not enjoy some duck shooting.

HOW A NATURAL FLIGHT-POND FORMED

Back in the days before the last war, the pool was little more than a trickle of water out of a rock fissure. Almost on the peak of the heather-covered Black Hill, it provided a welcome thirst-quenching drink, pure and sparkling, for the weary bilberry-picker or the ardent hiker.·To have referred to this tiny outlet as a pool would have been to invite ridicule. Scarely larger in area than the average goldfish pond, none could remember the time before it had existed. Likewise, none could recall when it had dried up, even in those glorious pre-war droughts: *'Man may come, and man may go, but I go on forever . . .'*

So it seemed with this crystal clear spring. Mountain sheep and animals of the wild watered there, and then came the Great Black Hill Fire of 1940, supposedly started by an irate farmer in an attempt to destroy the prolific rabbit population. The hill burned for a week, and then, amidst the scarred gorse, arising like some phoenix from the ashes, that spring bubbled steadily on. Back came the rabbits to drink from it, and apart from the blackened and scarred landscape, life reverted to normal. The heavy snows of winter, followed by the lush new growth of

131

spring, hid the horror of the previous August, and the locals forgot that there had even been a fire, except that the grouse were no longer to be heard.

Then with peace returning to the troubled countries of the world, the Forestry Commission came to the Black Hill. The winds of change were blowing, and before many months those six hundred acres of heather had come under the plough and crawler. Steep slopes were furrowed symmetrically, and conifer seedlings planted at intervals. 1953, as well as bringing that most dreaded scourge of all amongst the rabbit population, myxomatosis, saw a surprisingly rapid growth in the Black Hill thickets. A landscape that had earned its name from the dark purple of the heather was now the deep green of commercial forestry.

And that pool . . . welll, it had just bubbled on relentlessly throughout this manmade change, neither increasing nor decreasing, a trickling spring lost in a vast new forest. However, with the growth of the new timber, the threat of that which had once destroyed the old hill loomed more menancingly than ever . . . *fire!* Another inferno would be a thousand times more disastrous. Water was necessary in the event of flames ever surging over the Black Hill again. So, that tiny pool, and its surrounding slate bed, was transformed in the short space of a day into a hollow some fifteen yards long by ten wide. With that same unhurried trickle, the diverted spring flowed into its new outlet. It took less than a week to fill, a clear, cold pool to tempt any walker on a blazing hot summer's day.

Eventually, reeds grew around the side, and frogs croaked on still evenings, enhancing the initial scar made by man. Birds and beasts of the forest still drank there, and yet another era had begun.

This was how I found the pool when I first rented the shooting rights of the Black Hill. An ideal flight-pond? After several hundred-weight of barley had lain untouched in the shallows for weeks on end, I abandoned the idea of duck ever visiting this lonely place. Perhaps a pheasant in the reeds, but nothing more. It was altogether too remote.

Suddenly, one afternoon, some three months later, when a thin layer of snow covered the surrounding hills, I was surprised by a gutteral quacking, and the sunlight glinting on the blue/green sheen of mallards as five of these birds struck up at my approach. It was more by luck than judgement that I secured a right and left, and even as my labrador retrieved the second bird, I was already wondering whether a chance

132

8-1   A woodland pool that was once only a small spring: nature was transformed in a mysterious way.

(photo: Guy Smith)

bunch of passing mallard had alighted here, or if this had been their intended destination since departing from waters unknown.

In the weeks that followed, mallard were seen regularly on this small pond, but February 1st being past, the gun remained silent. Indeed, I would have had it no other way, for their presence alone was an achievement undreamed of.

Another season, and September and October yielded five mallard to a hundredweight of barley. Then during November and December the night sky was silent, and no whistling wingbeats nor gutteral quackings were to be heard.

Then in January, the duck were back again, and before the season had closed I had accounted for another ten. The hardened duck-shooter will scoff at a total of fifteen mallard in a season, but he would have to visit this delightful little pond personally to understand what I mean. The size of the bag counts for nothing.

So, a routine developed as far as this seemingly inconspicuous, yet none the less charming, woodland pool was concerned. The duck came in September, and continued to flight in nightly almost to the end of October, when they disappeared until the New Year arrived. Where did they go, or, most intriguing of all, whence did they come? A study of an ordnance survey map of the area did little to unravel the mystery for there was no sizeable lake or river within a radius of five miles. Perhaps to solve it would spoil it, for these two unanswered questions add much to the appeal of my tiny flight-pond.

Has the landscape, which man has changed so drastically, brought all this about? Certainly the duck would never have flighted to that bubbling spring of pre-war days. Does my pond lie *en route* to their night feeding grounds, or has the newly grown forest caused them to change their route?

These mysteries will go unsolved, and that is the way I would prefer it, but for how long will this convenient and exciting state of affairs last in this ever-changing world where progress has priority?

IMPROVING A WOODLAND POOL

Much has been written in the past concerning the construction and maintenance of artificial flight-ponds, but scant attention has been paid to the small woodland pool in a remote area which has prospects of good duck-shooting, merely requiring perseverance on the part of the owner or tenant. The secret of success with any flight pool is making the area of water at your disposal sufficiently *attractive* for duck to favour it in preference to other alternatives.

One of the main curses of woodland pools is *algae*, that floating weed which appears on stagnant water about mid-summer, and persists until the first frosts. The recommended treatment for this is a pond weedkiller by the name of algaemycin, but the amount required to treat an average pool, containing 30,000 gallons of water, is hard on the pocket of the shooting man. It would amount to something in the region of £20 for one application, and two, or even three, may be necessary in order to clear it completely. The preparation is designed primarily for the treatment of ornamental fishponds.

However, I invested in enough to treat my own pool once, and, working strictly to the instructions, with a hand-operated crop-sprayer, I sprayed the total area of water. The result was that much of the weed died, but a spell of hot weather, a fortnight or so later, caused another growth, and before long I was back where I started.

I had more or less decided, when September came, that I would not be able to start any duck-shooting until the frosts arrived. Then, suddenly, one day I disturbed ten mallard off the very thickest part of the weed. As a result I decided to feed my pool, tipping barley into the shallows, and watching the grain sink beneath the thick green mass until it was no longer visible from above. For the next few weeks I enjoyed some first class sport, the mallard and occasional teal flighting in regularly to my algae-covered pond.

I think one of the most attractive features, from a duck's point of view, about woodland pools is the shelter from the elements. They have not the discomfort of riding out a gale on an exposed expanse of water, not trying to hold their own against the fast-running current of a river. The atmosphere is comparatively still, and they can feed in peace.

ATTRACTING DUCKS

The two main ways in which to maintain a regular flow of incoming duck to such a pond is:

1. To keep it well fed.
2. Not to overshoot it.

Only a limited number of duck, those which have discovered this little 'snug', will be using it, as opposed to a similar pool situated on a regular flight-line or near to the coast where passing birds will notice it, and perhaps drop in out of curiosity more than anything else. I always like to hear duck going in to my pool after I have packed up, and crept stealthily away. I distinctly remember one occasion on which I sat out a flight on my own pool. Dusk deepened to darkness, and then a glorious full moon rose. I left then, for I fully believe that moonlight shooting upsets any small pool. As I reached my car, a hundred yards or so away, I heard that magical whisper of wingbeats above me, and, looking up I saw two mallard, silhouetted against the moon, heading for the pool. They would be there another day.

Like small pools, the woodland pond, particularly one at a high altitude, will become frozen over whenever there is a hard frost. One accepts this enforced break during the shooting season, and it may benefit the duck-shooter in the long run. If he has been over-zealous, then he will be compelled to give his birds a break. Yet, duck need not necessarily be prevented from flighting in just because of a sheet of ice. My own method of retaining the continuity of flighting duck is to tip loads of potatoes into the shallows so that they protrude above water level, in the form of an extension of the bank. The frost will break these open, and soften them in the manner in which the hungry duck like them. Some gamekeepers and shooting men boil potatoes for their flight-ponds, but I prefer to let the frost do the work for me. I have, on several occasions, stood quietly in the surrounding woodlands on a freezing cold night, and watched as many as a dozen mallard dropping in for a quick feed on these potatoes, before taking off back whence they had come.

WOODCOCK

Naturally, we associate woodland pools primarily' with duck-flighting, and possibly the odd cock pheasant foraging in the reed-beds. Yet, there is one bird whose presence here, from time to time, will be more than welcome—*the woodcock!* The sceptic will reply that these birds would probably be found within the surrounds of the woodlands, anyway. Possibly so, but I have shot more woodcock *flighting in* to my pool than I have elsewhere. It was some time before I actually discovered their interest in my pool. Actually, it was not the pool, but the heaps of rotting potatoes which were the main attraction. I have no

8-2   Woodcock provide excellent sport attracted by the woodland pool.
(Anthea Hadley from a drawing by Bob Sanders)

doubt that certain insects were to be found in there which were very much to the liking of these long-billed birds of mystery. The duck-shooter would do well to note that in order to shoot these birds he needs to hold a game licence, and also that their close season ends on September 30th, not August 31st, as for duck.

In many ways he who shoots a woodland pool is more fortunate than his counterpart on larger stretches of water in less remote areas, or the coastal gunner. There is an air of peace about the whole setting, and he has the whole place to himself. If he hears duck in the sky above, then he can be almost certain that they are coming to *his* pool. There will be nobody in close proximity to take a hurried long range shot, or to show an upturned face, and frighten them off. All that is required is patience.

It is up to the man who owns, or has the shooting rights over, one of these secluded pools to shoot it sparingly, *and to maintain it as a wild-fowl sanctuary* throughout the rest of the year. Not only will he benefit from it, but so will other shooting men for miles around, and, of course, the duck themselves. A woodland pool can be your very own Nature Reserve.

BUILDING A FLIGHT-POND

In many cases an artificial flight-pond can be as effective as a natural one, but before we attempt its construction some thought must be given to its siting.

A pool should always be sited where it can be seen from the air by ducks passing over. One that is hidden away in some corner of the shoot is likely to be visited only by those birds which know about it, and many mallard and teal will fly over without even being aware of its presence.

An elevated pool is generally preferable to one in a valley, although the latter may be easier to construct, particularly if there is a stream nearby which can be used to fill it. One must remember, however, that it is an offence to dam up a natural stream, and one's deed will surely be discovered in a few days when some farmer lower down becomes aware that the flow of water which feeds his cattle-drink has dried up. It is perfectly in order, though (with the landlord's permission), to widen the banks of a stream to form a pool, and possibly permission may be obtained from those farmers across whose land it flows, to dam the stream *temporarily* whilst your own pool fills up. Perhaps the dam can

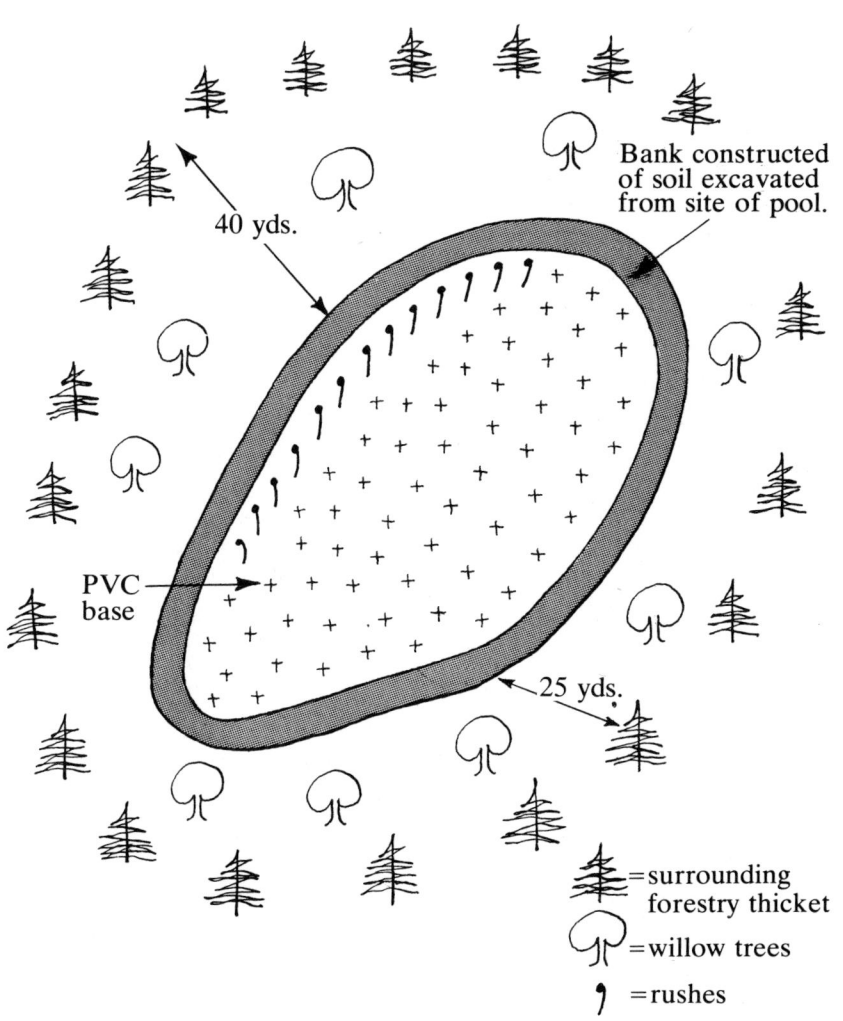

8-3   Constructing an upland flight-pond

even be left in place permanently providing that the water flows on over the top of it. All that you have actually done is widen the stream in one place.

A dam needs to be secure in order to be effective. It is no use merely blocking the watercourse with soil and stones from the existing bank. Bricks are best, and they will be that much more effective if a few are cemented together into sections beforehand. This forms the base, and once you have blocked the majority of the watercouse you can then fill in with soil, banking it up behind your existing dam.

Flight-ponds, generally, should be shallow, and need be no more than a foot deep in any place. The edges can be as little as four or five inches, and it is into these that you will tip barley. Duck like to dabble in shallow water, and will often avoid deep ponds for this reason.

As we have seen, a pool is easier to make in a valley than higher up in the hills, but success in the seasons ahead will depend on individual areas. However, our main concern is the making of a pool up in the hills.

The Forestry Commission are usually only too happy to have an abundance of water on their land amidst vast plantations where there is always the risk of fire. Nevertheless, their permission must be sought before starting work, and providing that it does not interfere with growing timber this will probably be given. We are faced with a tract of land on which there is no convenient stream, and not only must we sight our pool to its best advantage, but we must also take steps to see that it holds water at all times.

A mechanical digger is necessary in the beginning for in the majority of upland regions there is a bed of hard rock or slate beneath the soil. These machines can be hired quite economically, for the work involved in digging out a pool of average size, say thirty yards by ten yards, will be completed in a few hours. It will certainly be an investment.

Choose the largest clearing you can find for your site. It is as well if the surrounding trees are some distance away because duck are always wary of the possibility of a lurking enemy, and if the plantation comes right up to the banks they will be inclined to shun the pool for fear of foxes lying in wait under such convenient cover. Do not regard the woods in the proximity as hides. If necessary build some out in the open. Shooting from trees is very restrictive, and many a shot is spoiled by overhanging foliage.

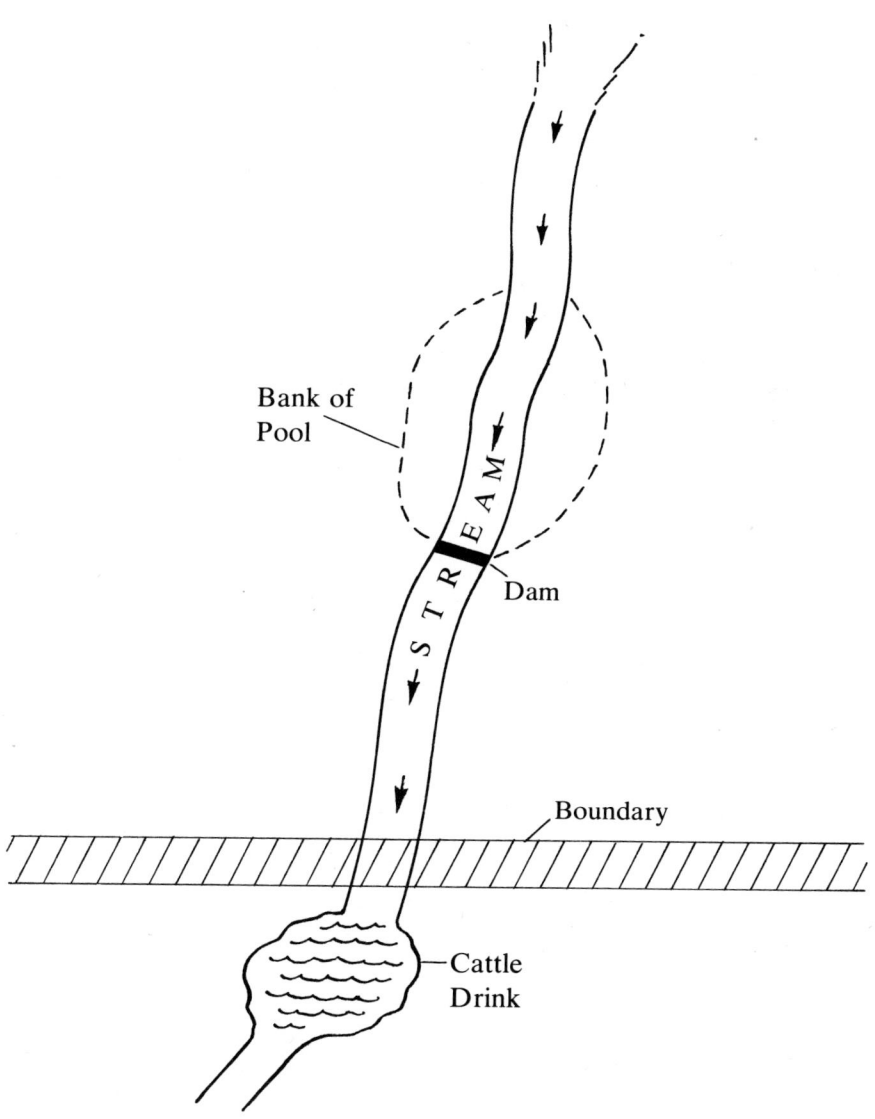

Bank of
Pool

S T R E A M

Dam

Boundary

Cattle
Drink

8-4   Constructing a Flight-pond on a stream

141

Your pool is dug out, and now you must take steps to make sure that it holds water. A lining of PVC sheeting is ideal, held down with rock, and it can also be covered with soil if necessary. The Forestry Commission use this material for lining their own artificial reservoirs.

The soil dug out can be used to make a surrounding bank, and the pool will soon lose its artificial look if you plant clumps of heather and gorse on it, and perhaps even sow grass seed.

COVER

Whilst a bare pool in the midst of the woods will certainly draw the odd duck or two, it will be vastly improved by the planting of *natural* cover round about. Reeds will provide the cover which duck like on a pool, somewhere in which to skulk when danger threatens, and the birds will feel much more secure here than when feeding on open water. Likewise, you will often find mallard or teal on there during the daylight hours.

Willows are all part of the scene, and one or two of these strategically placed will provide one with ideal hides from which to shoot.

A pool takes time to settle and blend into its natural surroundings, and one must not look for overnight success. With PVC sheeting as a base your pool will hold water and only dry up during times of drought. Constant feeding will provide the necessary attraction for the duck, but the greatest mistake is *over-shooting*. No pool should be shot more than once a fortnight, and in the very early stages after the building of the pond it is inadvisable to shoot it at all. You have not created an instant duck decoy with which to stock your freezer. You have invested in regular duck-shooting which will go on, hopefully, for several years. Do not abuse it. 'Feed regularly and shoot sparingly' should be your motto.

CHAPTER 9

Pigeons: the nucleus of the Hill-shooter's Sport

THE WOODPIGEON

We are all familiar with the peaceful cooing of the woodpigeon. It has a soothing effect upon all who listen to it, and is in keeping with the tranquility of the countryside. It is a bird which we take for granted, yet today, in various parts of the country, it is not as numerous as we are inclined to think.

Over the years our resident woodpigeon population has been swelled during the winter months by migrant birds from the continent. During spells of hard weather immense damage has been done to fields of greenstuffs by the ravenous flocks. All out efforts, including a brief experiment with narcotics, failed to check the marauders. However, during the last two or three winters the woodie has been conspicuous by its scarcity. Only in certain areas has pigeon control been necessary. A succession of mild winters has been responsible for this. Only in the severest weather, when sprouts or broccoli peeping through the snow are the only available food, will the woodpigeon resort to ravaging crops on this scale. It shows a preference for clover, and whilst this is attainable it will feed almost unnoticed.

Mild winters on the continent mean that the flocks in those countries have no need to migrate. So, it seems, everybody is happy. The woodie is content because he has ample food, and the farmer is relieved that his crops are left unmolested. However, it has been reported in sporting journals recently that the pigeon is on the decline. A price of 40p. per bird being offered by exporters, at a time of writing, has been blamed. Is it that the continentals have shot and eaten all their own birds, and now have need of ours? I doubt it very much. I am more inclined to believe that the bird is more evenly distributed, and concentrations of flocks are not so frequent.

Let us take a look at the bird in question. The woodpigeon is shy and gentle. Its voracious appetite is its only shortcoming. Once the winter is over its thoughts turn to nesting at the first hint of warm weather. Thousands are caught out when winter returns with a vengeance, but they persevere. The nest is a flimsy affair, and often a thick bush is chosen in preference to a nearby tree. Two eggs are laid, white in colour, and a walk through one's nearest woodland, anytime between April and August, will reveal the odd empty shell lying on the ground. Usually, this is the work of the predatory corvine tribe. I have found eggs in a nest as late as November. The woodpigeon does not believe in wasting breeding time!

The fledglings are ugly, and it is often difficult to believe that they will grow into the handsome grey bird which we know so well. At this stage they are vulnerable to winged predators, especially the sparrow-hawk, also increasing in numbers lately, and a cluster of scattered feathers beneath the trees usually means that this bird has struck.

The crop of the woodpigeon has an amazing capacity. I have seen as much as two handfuls of grain or greenstuff removed from a dead bird. Its method of feeding is to eat greedily for several hours, until the crop is full to bursting point, when it retires to rest and digest. Feeding begins at daylight, followed by a short 'day roost' in a convenient wood four or five hours later. This is followed by another spell of intense feeding prior to roosting shortly before dusk.

One item on the pigeon's menu that is not generally known is the bilberry. These berries are consumed long before they ripen, but are detected by a discolouration of the droppings. Blackberries, to a lesser extent are eaten, but usually only when they are fully ripe and juicy. These figure in the early autumn diet, but not at the expense of more satisfying foodstuffs.

There is something traditionally British about the cooing of the woodpigeon, and the loud flap of its wings as it breaks cover. I am sure that it is a bird which will hold its own for a long time to come in this ever-changing countryside of ours.

SPORT AT ITS FINEST

I had never really considered the prospect of shooting pigeons seriously on my hill shoot. Admittedly, I had used decoys from time to time over the years, but this had only been on the odd occasion when

Plate 4

Top : A Pool in the Hill — Ideal for Duck Flighting
Bottom : Young Pheasants Just Released into Cover

the birds were in a particular area, perhaps frequenting a belt of oak trees in search of acorns, or a field of stooked corn. Yet the vey idea of a full scale operation in early May, using camouflage netting, lofting poles, and a van load of impedimenta, seemed so uncharacteristic of the very surroundings, presenting a challenge so unique that we determined to have a go.

We had spotted the woodies a fortnight or so ago, on a field in the valley way below my shoot, gorging themselves on ten acres of lush clover. Without the aid of a pair of binoculars they would have been practically invisible from my woods, but noticing the regularity with which the pigeons were flighting over a particular corner of my shoot in the early evening, my companion and I did some reconnaissance work, and made a few plans. We decided there and then to exploit the situation to the best of our ability.

Thus, two weeks later, the earliest opportunity which presented itself, found us on the edge of the woods overlooking the feeding pigeons, half a mile or so below. It was mid-day, so we had plenty of time to prepare for the flight which we anticipated would begin about 4.30 p.m. There was a strong wind blowing from the birds to us which was a definite advantage, for the sound of shots would not be heard by those following on. On the other hand, it would make for decidely tricky shooting on the steep hillsides, the pigeons having the wind in their tails.

Two very large home-made decoys were lofted on to the top of a tall dead tree, and then another half-dozen or so were perched along the outskirts of the Forestry Commission thicket, giving an overall very lifelike picture from a pigeon's point of view. A hide was constructed by means of hanging a large section of camouflage netting across some bushes *outside* the woods, thus giving us unrestricted vision, and complete freedom of movement, two factors so vital for good shooting.

It was now 1.45 p.m. Pigeons were still flying in to feed on the distant clover field, and judging that we had at least another three hours before they started to flight back to their roosting grounds, I decided to leave my colleague "on guard" in the hide, and go on my weekly tour of inspection of my shoot. As I set off, I could not have wished for a more peaceful environment. The sun shone out of a cloudless blue sky, and the birds sang, rejoicing in the fact that every vestige of winter had now disappeared. A cock pheasant was shouting somewhere in the depths of the forest, and I caught a glimpse of a henbird slinking into the under-

145

9-1 A Pigeon-shooter; well camouflaged, on a day when hill fog is to his advantage.

(photo: Lance Smith)

9-2   Pigeon Shooting in a Panoramic Setting: careful planning is essential to maximize results.

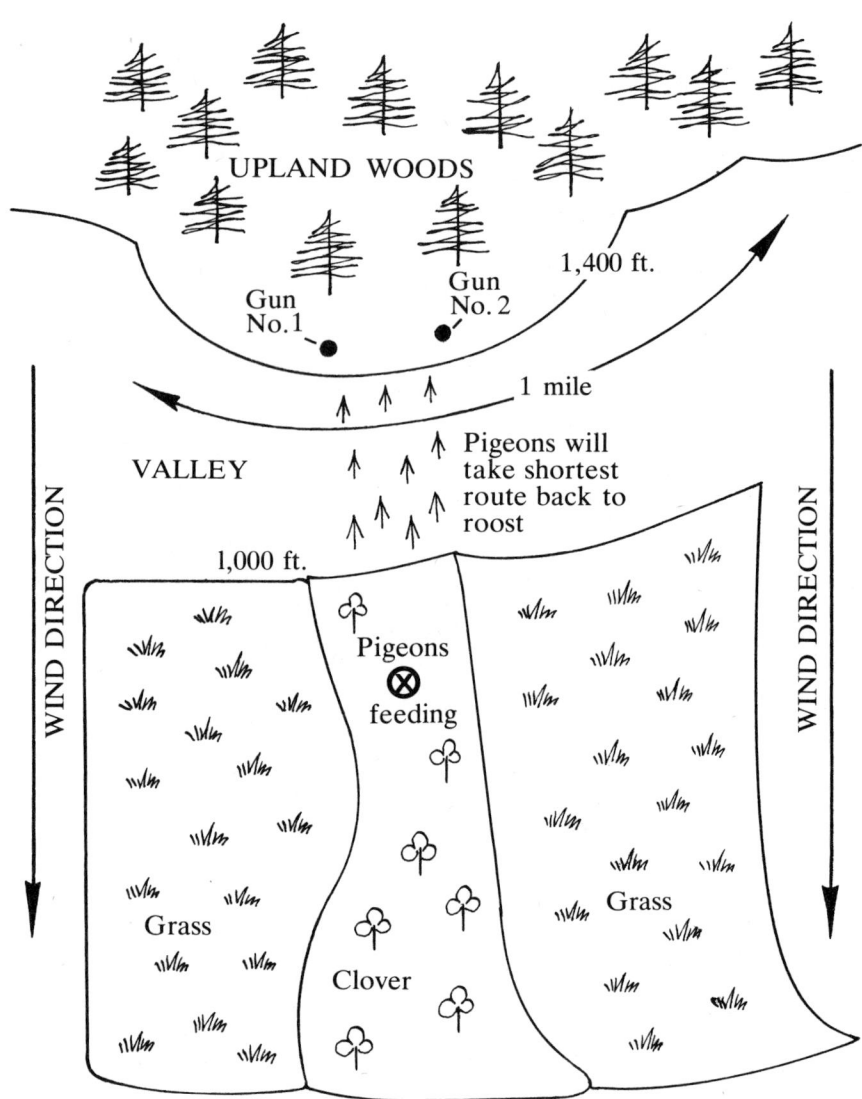

9-3 Pigeon Shooting Diagram (in the Hills when conditions
are favourable).

growth out of my way. From the heather slopes beyond a curlew warbled, and a pair of mallard quacked, almost lazily, off the small woodland pool, as I surprised them feeding on the remnants of the ton of potatoes which I had dumped there last season. A little further on I shot a couple of rabbits. Normally I would have left them alone at this time of the year, but nowadays complaints begin flooding in once they begin to breed, even in small numbers, so consequently I am forced to shoot them at every opportunity.

It was 4.20 p.m. before I was back in the hide. Those pigeons were still going down to feed, but none had yet shown the slightest signs of flying back to roost. We ate our tea as we watched the grey horde devouring theirs greedily, and suddenly we spotted a movement in the adjoining field. At first we mistook it for a hare, but as it loped away from the hedgerow there was no doubt that it was a fox, most probably a vixen in search of food for her cubs. She circled the sheep field, possibly hoping to find a dead or sick lamb, but having no such luck, she disappeared into a small spinney on the brow of the hill where there was a possibility of surprising an unwary rabbit.

One of the things which amazed me most during that long vigil was the apparent calmness with which the feeding pigeons viewed a buzzard which hovered above them. So often have I seen woodpigeons fleeing as though the devil himself was on their tails, at the appearance of one of these large birds of prey, yet now they took not the slightest notice of this, one of their natural enemies. I can only conclude that either they felt there was safety in numbers, or else their clover field was far too luscious to forsake just because one buzzard came to have a look at them.

At 6.35 p.m. the last two pigeons went down to feed. I began to wonder if they were ever going to move. The wind was strengthening fast, and now that the warmth had gone out of the sun's rays, I was glad that I had brought my thick polo-necked sweater with me.

At 6.45 p.m. the first shot was fired as the pigeons began to stream back to the woods. High and fast they came, and it took us about a dozen misses before we realised that each hurtling grey bird required almost double the normal amount of forward allowance. We were firing as fast as we could reload for the next ten minutes, and rather than lament the thirty or so pigeons which we missed in a true sporting fashion, I would prefer to compliment my friend upon the four which he killed

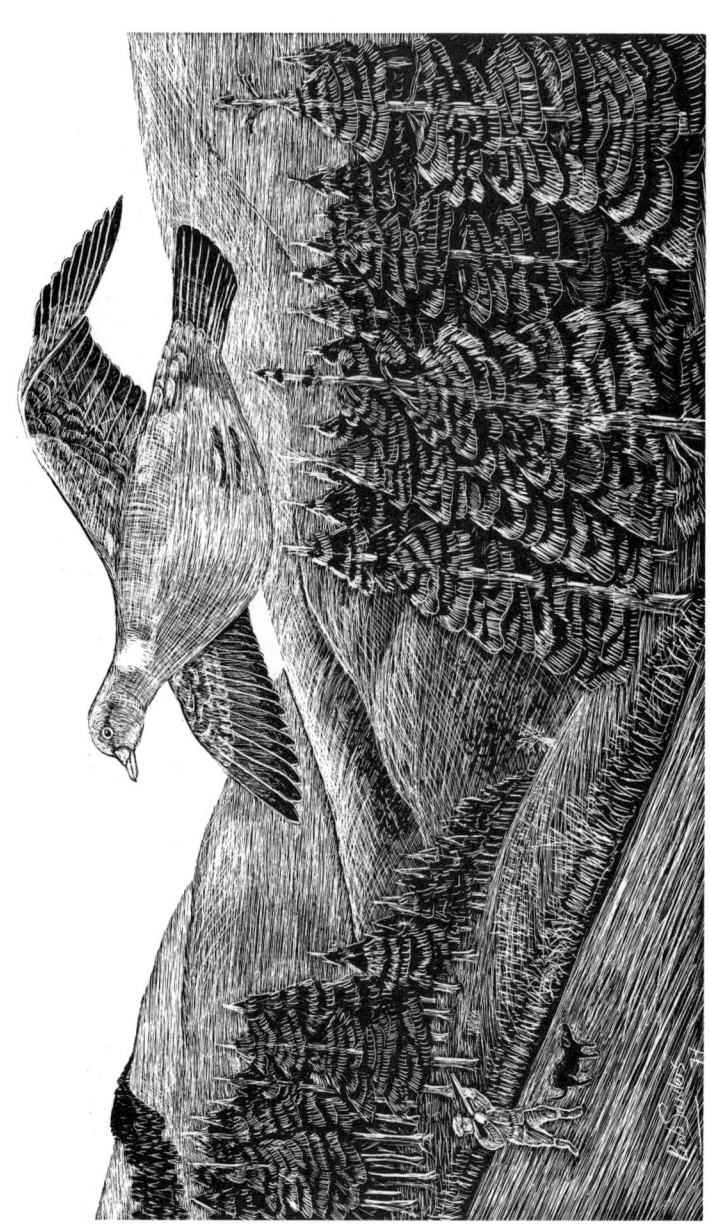

9·4 "The First Shot was Fired". The pigeon returning to roost.   (Drawing by Bob Sanders)

killed cleanly and in fine style.

Suddenly it was all over, and we stood looking across the empty panoramic landscape below us. Not a pigeon was in sight, and only the lone buzzard wheeled effortlessly above the slopes of the valley. Perfect peace reigned once again after our hectic barrage. Many would say that it had all been a complete waste of time, but I would disagree with them. The size of the bag in no way reflected the pleasure and anticipation which had been ours for the greater part of that day, something which is of far greater importance when shooting pigeons in such conditions.

CHAPTER 10

Foxes and Fox Clubs

FOX CONTROL

The fox is the sworn enemy of all hill farmers. Whilst the sportsman has every admiration for this cunning foe, the flockmaster is forced to take a more practical view. Losses of lambs and poultry can cost him dearly, and as a result war is waged upon Reynard in a variety of ways. His stronghold, the thickly wooded hills, are often impenetrable, and the vixen can rear her cubs with almost total immunity.

Traditonal fox-hunting is hampered by the terrain, and in spite of frequent meetings by the hunt, the quarry nearly always has the advantage. Seldom is he pursued across open country. A short run, a few twists and turns amidst the plantations, and he has thrown off his pursuers.

Snaring is possibly the most effective method of controlling an ever-increasing fox population in the hills, and almost every farmer maintains a network of wires set in gaps in hedges and fences on his land. Many foxes are accounted for in this way, but the shooting tenant will only seldom obtain a shot at a fox during his sporting forays. Often it is a snap shot as a surprised, possibly careless, fox bolts for the nearest patch of cover.

The scent of a fox is unmistakeable, a sharp unpleasant odour which hangs in the atmosphere for sometimes as long as half an hour when this creature has been lying up in a particular place on a windless day.

There are a number of Fox Clubs situated throughout the majority of our remote hill areas. Their main object is *sport* as well as a free service provided to farmers and game-preservers. Whenever I am approached by one of these clubs I am only too happy for them to arrange a foray on my own shoot. Seldom is permission refused for them to enter any tract of land in the hills, and having accompanied them on several

10-1   A Humane Fox-trap: designed and made by Fred Ellett,
and proved to be successful.

(photo: Lance Smith)

occasions I am impressed by their efficiency.

The beaters consist mainly of sons (and daughters!) of these hill folk, youngsters who are willing to force their way through the thickest possible undergrowth, and sometimes crawl on hands and knees beneath fir thickets. They are accompanied by the men with the terriers, surely the bravest of all dogs, yapping excitedly, and then breaking into full cry when they get a fresh scent.

The more guns available, the better, but some forethought must be given to their placing, as in dense cover *safety is of paramount importance.* Most Forestry Commission woods are divided up into plantations, separated by either slate roads or fire-breaks. The guns should be positioned at fifty yard intervals along these, all standing on the same side of the ride in order to eliminate any dangerous crossfire. Silence is essential, and concentration must not be allowed to lapse, for a fox is capable of crossing a narrow track in a couple of bounds when it is lost to sight in the opposite thicket. It is essential that each covert is entirely surrounded by guns throughout the respective drives.

Each drive may take up to an hour, depending upon the size of the plantations, but the beaters and terriers must be allowed time to traverse the ground thoroughly. If the beating force is insufficient in numbers, often foxes will circle round and return to cover *behind* the dogs.

After each drive everybody must assemble for a brief post-mortem. Sometimes weather conditions can have an adverse effect upon prior planning, and a change of wind direction may result in an alternative method of driving the next beat. The beaters should always walk *with* the wind, their intention being to let any fox become aware of their presence, and drive it towards the guns.

At one recent such drive no fewer than twelve foxes were flushed from a twenty-acre plantation! Unfortunately on that particular day there was a scanty turn-out of guns, and only one fox was shot. On the very same territory, three weeks later, six foxes were found, three of which were shot.

A bright sunny day is best for fox-driving in this manner. Snow, provided it is not deep enough to hinder the beaters, gives a better indication of the tracks which the foxes are using. A point worth remembering is that foxes, like rabbits, invariably bolt *uphill.* This should only be taken as a vague guide, though, and guns must be stationed on the lower reaches of a hillside as well. The fairest method

155

10-2   A Vixen Caught In Late January.

(photo: Lance Smith)

10-3   Lambs Are Always In Danger From Foxes.

(photo: Guy Smith)

is to draw lots for positions. Wherever you are, though, there is *always* the chance of a shot, so it never pays to relax your vigilance.

It is an unwritten law amongst fox shooters in the hills that the man who kills a fox claims it, no matter on whose land it was shot. Carcases are usually placed in the lower branches of nearby trees until the shoot is over, for if the terriers seize them, the pelts (which if skinned and dried properly sell at about fifteen pounds each), will be pulled apart. Mostly these clubs sell the skins, and pool the rewards at the end of the season.

Terriers are not necessarily the only breed of dog which will drive foxes successfully. I was most impressed on one occasion by the efforts of a sheepdog, accompanying the terriers. This dog followed a wounded fox into thick cover and held it at bay until two of the guns arrived on the scene.

The fox enjoys a unique status in hill country, a hated enemy, but at the same time a worthy quarry. Once I was inclined to regard fox-driving as somewhat unsporting, but having sampled it in the manner in which it is conducted in the hills, I have totally changed my mind. I would advocate it as the most humane method of control, but would stress that no shot-size smaller than BB should be used, and foxes must not be fired on at distances of more than 35 yards. Clean kills are our aim. No true sportsman wishes to see a wounded fox dragging itself into cover to die a lingering death, perhaps days later.

THE 'BLACK FOX'

Foxes vary in colour, some darker, some lighter than the average reddish-brown one. Likewise, almost every tract of hill country has a fox that is easily distinguishable from its fellow creatures, and it is at once regarded as having more cunning and tenacity than its brethren. Any particular raids of outstanding audacity and ferocity are at once attributed to this 'rogue fox', whether or not the creature in question is actually responsible. Each farmer, or member of a Fox Club, is anxious to secure its pelt and claim the credit. Perhaps only those directly associated with hill sport can understand this. I certainly can, for I came up against such a fox, although I would have wished a more glamorous fate upon it, a charge of BB shot bowling it over in full flight as it sought to penetrate a line of guns, or pulled down by a pack of zealous hounds after a long chase across open country. But it was not to be.

I first came across the 'black fox', as we eventually came to call him,

10-4   The work of foxes: a grim reminder that control is essential.

(photo: Guy Smith)

in the spring of 1970. I was patrolling my shoot when I saw him coming across one of the adjoining sheep fields, trotting with an arrogance which in itself was a defiance of the nearby farmers, and all those whose hands were against him. I noted at once the colour of his fur, so dark that he seemed to be almost jet black from a distance, except for the distinctive white markings on the tip of his tail and his forelegs. I was fully two hundred yards from him, but he spotted me almost at once. Probably, he had picked up my scent for the wind was blowing towards him. Suddenly, he stopped, and as he did so, I noticed that he was carrying something in his mouth, something brown and fluffy, from which clusters of feathers were wafting away in the breeze. It was a fowl, stolen from one of the farms in broad daylight. The fox looked in my direction, hesitated, as though trying to decide whether or not it was worthwhile changing direction, and then, with a sudden movement, he disappeared through a hole in the hedge, and was lost to sight in some nearby gorse bushes.

During the next few weeks this animal began to build up a reputation for himself amongst the surrounding hill farmers and shepherds. His audacity was outrageous, yet the swiftness and unexpectedness of his daylight raids on poultry rendered him immune to the threat of guns which were kept in readiness for him. On one particular farm he escaped with no fewer than four barnyard hens in one week, and, just when everybody was anticipating that he would put in another daylight appearance, he changed his predatory rambles to the nocturnal hours. There is always the stubborn rooster which prefers the thorn bush in the paddock to the safety and comfort of the hen-house, and Reyanard's larder did not go short.

When summer arrived, little was seen of the marauding fox. Probably, he was lying up close to his vixen somewhere, preferring the easy prey of young rabbits to the hazards of running the gauntlet of the farms. However, the hill farmers had not forgotten their vows of vengeance, and many a rusty old hammer-gun was kept permanently in the outhouses in readiness for when their sworn enemy next put in an appearance.

Reynard was not seen again until the fall of the leaf when hunting began in earnest. On the day in question, I was following the hounds on foot across the rugged terrain, when suddenly I heard them baying, and saw a fox in full flight, some two hundred yards ahead of his pursuers,

10-5   A Fox-club Breaks For Lunch: only one kill made during three morning drives.

(photo: Lance Smith)

in open country. I felt my pulses quicken when I recognised the hounds' quarry—none other than the black fox. They were gaining on him, too, and now the distance separating them was less than 75 yards. Then, when the leading hound was virtually snapping at his trailing bush, Reynard made the safety of the vast Forestry Commission woods, impenetrable thickets where he was familiar with every square foot of ground. Seconds later, both fox and hounds had disappeared from my sight, and I was left to follow their progress by the incessant baying which came to me on the wind.

Of course, they lost him. Any huntsman who has attempted to draw these densely planted fir-plantations knows that the odds are well in favour of the fox. Yet, later that night, when I called in at Farmer Jones' for a chat, and a cup of tea, he told me that he had seen the 'outlaw fox', as he called him, emerging quite unconcernedly from out of the grounds of a nearby disused chapel, just as dusk was falling, a plump white duck clamped firmly in his wicked jaws! Had he decided that the safety of consecrated ground was preferable to the deep woods after all?

My next meeting with the black marauder came shortly after Christmas when I was out with a couple of colleagues on my shoot, endeavouring to bag a brace of pheasants, and perhaps a mallard or two, if we were lucky. As we stealthily approached my small flight-pond amongst the fir woods, the sound of furious splashing, flapping of wings, and alarmed quacking, reached our ears from the surrounding reeds. I was puzzled, for a mallard which quacks in such a fashion usually loses no time in taking to the wing, and escaping from the scene of its disturbance. As we crept nearer, the rushes on the opposite side suddenly parted, and we had a fleeting glimpse of a familiar dark-coated shape, bounding up the grassy bank beneath the shelter of the Corsican pines, a mallard quacking in panic held in its mouth, and a trail of blue, green, and brown feathers floating in its wake.

The depredations of the black fox continued up until February 1972. I saw him several times during the two years when he terrorised the game and poultry within his chosen territory. Worthy foe as he was, the hill farmers no longer regarded him as a sporting challenge, but set out to destroy him in any way they could. Snares were set in all gaps in hedgerows, and several foxes were accounted for (as well as a couple of ewes!) but the much sought after quarry remained at large. Drives were organised throughout all the woodlands, with teams of beaters and dogs

10-6   A Sheepdog: he worked well along with the terriers.
(photo: Lance Smith)

hoping to push the black fox into range of the waiting line of guns, but always they drew a blank. Twice he eluded the hunt, almost effortlessly, as though he was enjoying the chase as much as the huntsmen.

However, his day had to come some time. Farmer Johnson, returning from visiting some friends, in the early hours of one Sunday morning in late February, was speeding through the narrow lanes in his Land Rover. High hedges touched the vehicle on both sides, as he took some of the bends at an alarming rate. Suddenly, something moved in his path. His foot touched the brake pedal. A dog? A cat? Then it was only yards away, the twin beams of the headlights reflecting the dark sheen of its coat, interspersed with reddish brown, and two shining green eyes reflecting surprise and fear. Seconds later came the impact.

I inspected Reynard's body in Tom Johnson's barn the following morning. It was certainly a dark one, the black fur predominating, making the fox's natural colour almost inconspicuous. With my good friend's permission I removed the flowing brush, peeling it from the tail-bone, and later cured it with white spirit. It hangs in my study to this day, a tribute to a worthy foe, despite what those hill farmers might have to say, and my only regret is that the outlawed animal did not meet a more noble end, rather than death by misadventure.

Foxes are an integral part of life on the hills. Without them the natural environment would be incomplete. Our aim must always be control, and not extermination. They have their place amongst Nature's creatures, and play their own part in maintaining a balance, regardless of their depredations amongst game and livestock.

FOXHUNTING

Having discussed the ways by which the amateur gamekeeper can control foxes on his land we must not overlook the occasional visits of the local Hunt. Most huntsmen will admit that in upland regions, where the terrain consists mainly of thick woodlands, steep slopes, and dense patches of gorse, their kills throughout the season are much lower than those of packs which hunt over arable farmland. Nevertheless, they love their sport just as much and if we are to enjoy good relationships with them then we should allow them access to our land. In fairness to both parties, though, dates should be agreed upon well in advance. The coincidence of a shoot with a Hunt meeting will not please either party.

The fox certainly has the advantage in upland regions. He knows

10-7   The "Black Fox", a rascal who stole in the daylight.

(Anthea Hadley from a drawing by Bob Sanders)

every inch of the woods and hills, and once he enters those Forestry Commission plantations the hounds have little chance of catching up with him. However, the huntsmen in the Lake District pursue their quarry on foot, running and climbing behind a pack of hounds in full cry. Although their progress is slower they can travel where horses cannot, and they are much fitter as a result.

REMOVAL OF SNARES

It is only fair to the hounds that the gamekeeper takes up all his snares before a meeting of the local Hunt. Apart from the injury which might be inflicted upon a hound which becomes ensnared in full cry, these animals are costly, and the resulting vet's bill will be considerable. It is not sufficient merely to knock the snares off their pegs. A noose lying flat on the ground is quite likely to tighten over a hound's foot as it passes over it. *Remove every wire.* And the only way to be certain that you have done so is to count your snares as you set them so that you know exactly how many you have on your land. The one which you overlook is quite likely to be the one which catches a hound.

Hill farmers will invariably welcome a meet, Not only is it yet another means of combating the enemy which endangers their lambs in the early part of the year, but it is also tradition. It is part and parcel of our rural heritage, and we must play an active part in it if we are to enjoy the co-operation of both farmers and huntsmen.

So extend a welcome to the Hunt, and make your land safe for them. The disturbance which they will cause you should be negligible.

CHAPTER 11

Badgers and Deer

BADGERS

Badgers are probably the species of wildlife most affected by the changes to landscape brought about by reafforestation. Some of their setts are as much as fifty years old, being used by one generation after another, remote and undisturbed until the advent of modern forestry. They have existed in age-old woods, and then, suddenly their mode of life has been shattered by the felling of the oak and beech trees, their homes churned up as the ground has been ploughed into symmetrical furrows, and young fir trees planted.

So, Brock has been forced to move, in many cases, seeking a new home. The new woods do not appeal to his way of life. Yet, on infrequent occasions he has been spared this inconvenience. So it was on my own hill shoot, although I had been tenant for some time before I discovered his stronghold. The grouse and blackgame conceded defeat, but Brock held his own.

For years the vast acreages of heather had been the habitat of grouse and blackgame, their growling calls being heard night and morning, on the slopes above the isolated farms. Rarely were they shot, the farmers expounding most of their energy in a constant battle to eke out a living on their barren homesteads, and living with the wind in their teeth the whole time. They had neither the time nor the inclination to walk these border hills after grouse or blackcock, perhaps shooting the odd bird for the table when a covey ventured closer to civilisation. It was on such an occasion that Farmer Grubb shot the last grouse on Black Hill, in August 1941. A few years later, after the cessation of hostilities, vast tree-planting operations were begun here by the Forestry Commission. The heather, the staple diet of these grand upland sporting birds, was sacrificed to make way for the Corsican and Scots Pine. The

11-1 Badger: a front view.

(photo: Calvin Williams)

11-2 Badger: from the rear.

(photo: Calvin Williams)

birds deserted their home in search of new pastures, either on the Long Mynd, or further afield to the hills of Radnorshire. Yet another battle had been lost.

However, on the far side of the Black Hill, within a matter of a few hundred yards of these alterations to an age-old landscape, another species of wildlife was fighting desperately to maintain its last stronghold. Standing gaunt and windswept on the steep hillside, above the olde-worlde village of Clungunford, was a spinney of giant oak and beech trees. Countless buffetings they had withstood from gales and blizzards. One massive oak, twisted and horrifically scarred, had survived the ravages of a midsummer electric storm, the lightening depriving it of its lush foliage, and reducing it to a blackened skeleton. Yet, it had lived, fighting desperately for its life, until, one day, green leaf sprouted again. Its resilience had won through. However, this survivor is no ordinary tree. Beneath its roots, travelling deep down into the hill, twisting and turning at right angles, is the entrance to one of the largest badger setts in these hills. There are no signs of Brock's excavations, though, for the rain, over the years, has washed the soil back into the ground. The casual observer might be forgiven for presuming that this mighty sett is now unoccupied, its late inhabitants having followed in the wake of the deserting grouse. A closer examination will reveal the deep gouges on the bark of these sentinel trees where the badgers have sharpened their claws daily. A keen eye will also note the well-used track which leads away into a nearby thicket of bracken and gorse. This is the 'toilet area' where these, the cleanest of all animals, go to avoid fouling their living quarters.

The badger, who shows a strong preference for old, well-established woods, has no love for the artificially planted Forestry Commission thickets. So, as the crawlers and ploughs moved closer to this isolated last stronghold, Brock must have been preparing for a strategic withdrawal. The mighty oaks and beeches would soon be gone, the maze of underground tunnels filled in, as drab uniformity destroyed something which had been there since long before the English/Welsh wars.

On and on advanced the march of progress, a ruthless tide of relentlessness. The historic spinney was living on borrowed time. Weeks became days, days became hours, and then, when all seemed lost, the advancing army was suddenly halted. The powerful plough, which was effortlessly burying the purple heather before it, suddenly grinded helplessly on a bed of slate. An inspection by forestry officials revealed this immovable surface to be extensive. Only quarrying would defeat it, and this would be of no benefit to them. The obstacle would have to be circumnavigated.

Thus, the giant trees and the badger colony beneath them were granted a reprieve. The spinney became an island amidst a deep green sea of conifer thickets, the latter serving as additional security for their privacy. The casual trespasser, who might interfere with an ancient way of life, would not make the trip, on hands and knees, beneath the low branches, in order to explore a hidden spinney. The badgers would be safe for many years to come.

So, one struggle for survival in a hostile world has earned a welcome truce. The grouse and blackgame were defeated, but Brock had won his fight. It is remote refuges, such as this, which determines the future of every species of our wildlife, and we must take steps to safeguard them wherever possible.

DEER

In the majority of Forestry Commission sporting leases the right to kill deer is specifically excluded. The 'culling' is left to wardens and rangers whose experience eliminates much cruelty which would otherwise arise. Although the law definitely states that these majestic creatures may not be shot with a rifle of smaller bore than .240, and shotguns may only be used with shot sizes Special SG or larger, there is always the possibility of a tenant who might be tempted to 'have a go' in a moment of excitement with an ordinary game load. The chances of a clean kill are remote. More likely wounding would occur, and the animal would die a terrible, lingering death.

Nowadays the Sika deer is spreading throughout the British Isles. Of Japanese origin, it is suited to woodland areas, whether upland or lowland. We are likely to meet up with it almost anywhere. Temptation will rear its head, as it did with myself in the following account, yet I know that in the end I would not have raised my gun to the creature in question. It was simply curiosity which prompted me to follow the spoor in the snow.

The morning was mild and damp as John and I loaded the shooting gear into the estate car. In fact, it looked like being one of those dreary, mid-December days when the woods and fields would have a depressing

11-3 A Mountain Ram: a wild specimen which may be shot (but see
text on danger of shooting domesticated hill sheep).
(Anthea Hadley from a drawing by Bob Sanders)

air about them. We should not feel inspired to walk further than necessary, and the odd pheasant, which we might chance to stumble upon, would be more inclined to favour the use of its legs than its wings. The woodpigeons, undoubtedly, would choose to remain in the day shelter of the impenetrable fir thickets, and the rabbits would prefer their sandy burrows to the cloying, damp undergrowth. Only Remus, my yellow labrador, showed any enthusiasm whatsoever, panting fiercely in the luggage compartment behind the rear seat, and smearing the back window with his nose. He whined, impatiently, from time to time, eager to be away from this drab suburban area, and to frolic in the freshness of those border hills.

Methodically, I checked our impedimenta, a vital procedure where a round trip of 140 miles is involved. Two guns, ample cartridges (we were both optimists!), game-bags, flasks, sandwiches, wellington boots, a towel with which to dry Remus, and a torch, in case of a mechanical breakdown on the return journey. Remus whined again.

"Well," John remarked, adjusting his spectacles, and checking that he had his cigarettes and lighter, "are we ready for off, then?"

"Just about," I replied, endeavouring to inject some enthusiasm into my voice, for his benefit. Up in the hills there is *always* a chance of meeting with the unexpected, regardless of conditions.

"There's too much low cloud about for my liking," he remarked, surveying the rows of uniform houses on the estate beyond the two fields which my house overlooked. "Just look at that television transmitter. You can only see a hundred feet or so of the whole mast!"

"Maybe," I was still attempting to generate an air of indifference towards the climatic situation, "but where we're going, a good seventy miles from here, conditions could be a whole lot different." I did not deem it wise to mention that, more often than not, the upland area of my shooting rights was enveloped in thick hill-fog on such days as these, limiting visability to fifteen or twenty yards.

The first twenty miles or so of our journey necessitated the constant use of the windscreen wipers, the damp air combining with the filth thrown up by other road-users to obscure my vision through the windscreen. Even when we reached open, low-lying countryside, the mist still seemed to be rolling in to meet us.

"Could be tricky coming back tonight, if this lot thickens," John commented.

11-4 A Deer: startled and on the move.

(Anthea Hadley from a drawing by Bob Sanders)

I deemed not to answer him, remembering a similar day, some three years ago, when the return journey of 70 miles had taken me approximately four hours.

However, once we had left Bridgnorth behind us, and the road began climbing, parallel to the Brown Clee, the atmosphere became appreciably colder. The absence of low cloud was noticeable at once, and above the distant mountain peaks we saw the weak rays of a December sun.

"I say!" John leaned forward, peering at the far range of hills. "That looks like snow up there!"

"Most probably," I smiled, sensing that it wasn't going to be such a bad day after all. "It's certainly gone a lot colder."

When we reached Craven Arms it became necessary to switch on the car heater. The slopes of the hills on our left were covered with snow, the sky had cleared, showing patches of blue amongst the sparse cloud, and the sunshine was now more prominent. A flock of woodpigeons, feeding in a nearby field of kale, clattered skywards at the approach of our vehicle, and then, wheeling round in a wide half-circle, began gliding back down to their disturbed meal. Crows dotted the whiteness of the upper sheepfields, and, way above the horizon, a buzzard soared, effortlessly, with scarecely a flap of its ragged, moth-like wings.

I was forced to engage a lower gear as the lanes we were travelling began rising again, much more steeply this time. There was less green to be seen on the fields now, the snow having fallen much more heavily up here. Another mile or so, and we were motoring on hard-packed snow, tyre marks showing where the occasional hill farmer, concerned over his sheep in a distant field, had used a Land Rover to inspect them.

We arrived at our destination shortly before mid-day. The hundreds of acres of Forestry Commission plantation had a festive atmosphere about them, the branches of the larch, spruce, and pine supporting the snow, resembling their artificial counterparts in the city stores, where cotton wool and tinsel glittered beneath an array of coloured lights. Yet, up here, Nature herself was presenting us with a far more spectacular display.

I pulled the car partially off the narrow lane by the wide gateway which bore the notice, "Authorised Vehicles Only." Above us stretched the vast Mortimer Forest, below us the Pen-y-Cwm valley.

Remus was leaping about in the back with excitement, eager to begin the forthcoming foray, so I let him out, watching him scamper in the pure white powdery substance, so different from the wet snow and slush of urban areas. We decided that we would have something to eat before starting out, in order to avoid wasting time in the midst of our excursion, for we wished to take full advantage of the daylight at our disposal.

Thus, having consumed our sandwiches and coffee, we set off through the wide gateway, and climbed the slippery track into the frozen world around us. Both of us found the snowy atmosphere exhilarating, completely destroying the lethargic disposition with which we had begun the day. It was as though we had stepped into a white fairyland, thousands of miles away from the mundane world in which we were forced to exist for the majority of our lives.

Silence. We stopped to listen, but there was not a sound to be heard. Nothing moved. It did not really surprise me, for, on previous forays such as this, I had noted the marked absence of wildlife. The reason, actually, was quite simple. The woodpigeons, at the first hint of hard weather, seek the comparatively warmer climate of the valleys below, except for the few who are reluctant to desert their coniferous thickets, returning to roost at dusk, although they are forced to forage further afield for their food. The rabbits remain in their burrows for much of the time, surviving on 'emergency rations', which consist of the bark of the nearest saplings. The pheasant, of course, will skulk in the hedgerows bordering the sheep fields, and only the industrious dog, with a keen nose, will flush him out. Thus, at first sight, it seemed as though we were the sole intruders in an empty white world.

Eventually, we came to the little woodland pool, situated in a small clearing in the heart of this dense forest. Usually, we would approach it with caution, anticipating the sudden rush of powerful wings beating on the brackish water amidst alarmed quacking, and the sunlight reflecting the blue and green sheen of the drake mallard as he climbed rapidly, seeking the safety which lay beyond the surrounding treetops. Sometimes this drake would be alone, disturbed at his solitary meal on the barley which I had tipped into the shallows. At other times there would be as many as seven or eight other duck there with him, sometimes even the odd teal, seeking the company of its larger cousins.

Yet, today, there was an unbroken stillness in this glade. There was

176

no shimmering of sunlight on water beyond the reed beds, only the dazzling whiteness of the thin layer of snow which covered the ice beneath it. The mallard would return another day, when the thaw came.

We stood there in silence, for it was almost as though we were forbidden to speak, in this land where nothing moved. Even Remus remained motionless except for the pendulum-like movement of his tail.

"What's this?" John, who was some ten yards or so away from me, was peering at something in the snow at his feet. "You haven't by any chance got any deer on your land, have you?"

"Deer?" I could not contain my surprise. "Why, no! The nearest deer to here are around Ludlow. The Forestry Commission reckon they're spreading, but it's a bit much to expect them up here."

"Well, there's been a deer through here. It's been to the pool to try and break the ice for a drink. Hasn't had much success, though. Come and see for yourself."

I joined my companion, and gazed, almost unbelievingly, at that which he showed me. It was true enough. There, leading from the nearby thickets, was a set of cloven hoof prints, clearly defined in the virgin snow. They made directly for the water's edge. The snow had been scraped back off the ice, which was scarred with chippings, obviously made by a hoof, desperately trying to break through to the water beneath. Then, failing in its endeavours, it had trotted off down the ridge, and away.

"Hmm," I really could not believe what I saw. "It certainly does look like a deer. Yet, I never thought they'd get up here just yet."

"Probably the hard weather has driven this one far afield in search of food and water," there was a tremor of excitement in John's voice. "Shall we follow it?"

"You can only shoot deer with a rifle!" My sporting instincts were uppermost.

"You're allowed to use buckshot loads," My colleague was not to be dissuaded. "I've got a couple of SGs in my pocket. I generally carry a couple. You never know what you might come across, foxes, geese . . . deer!"

I could feel the temptation working on my better instincts.

"Well," I deliberated, not wishing to appear too enthusiastic. "I suppose we *could* try and track it. There again, I expect it's miles away by now." This latter was a sop to my conscience. I doubted very much whether we would even catch sight of the creature. I hoped not, except perhaps a fleeting glimpse of it in the distance, well out of range.

John handed me an orange-coloured cartridge. I noted the arrow-head emblem and the letters 'SG' on the outer casing. I took it, and, opening the breech of my gun, I swopped it for the crimson-cased No. 4 shot in the choke barrel. I had partially succumbed to temptation. The chase was on.

Remus needed little bidding to follow the scent of the deer as we started off at a brisk pace down the ride. However, in spite of his eagerness, he kept veering from the spoor, and bounding through the piles of dead bracken in search of pheasants.

It was extraordinary how resolutely the deer kept to the straight forestry road, its tracks visible in the stretches of unbroken snow for as far as the eye could see. I would have thought that it would have preferred the comparative shelter and safety of the plantations of larch, spruce, and pine which bordered these slate roads.

On an on we went, covering milè after snowbound mile, hopefully following that line of cloven hoofprints, and the yellow labrador who never thought of slackening his pace for one moment. We were cold no longer. Indeed, the beads of perspiration stood out on our foreheads. I wished that I had not donned that extra sweater before starting out. I could always take it off, I reflected, but I would probably catch a chill, and, anyway, I should only have to carry it.

Suddenly, Remus halted. His tail was erect, and his nose sniffed the air. In front of him, just a yard or so off the path, was a gigantic mound of dead bracken, and the tracks led directly to it! Remus was motionless for the moment, but I knew full well that it was only a matter of seconds before he plunged into it.

I eased forward the safety catch on my gun, and held up a warning finger to John. He nodded his assent, and brought his own weapon up, holding it at the ready. For what seemed an eternity we were frozen into immobility, two men and a dog, all tensed, ready for the kill. The silence was even more noticeable.

Then Remus jumped. His leap, using his two powerful back legs as a lever, carried him into the very centre of this bed of dead vegetation, and with a crash that seemed to echo throughout the silent woodlands, he disappeared from our sight. We heard further threshings as he burrowed deeper into the ferns and brambles, and then with an ear-

178

splitting "cak-up-cak-up" something burst upwards, a blurr of wings propelling a reddish-brown body, the neck ringed with white.

"Pheasant!" I shouted unnecessarily, my surprise and panic evident in the way I mounted my gun to my shoulder. Four shots blasted the crisp air, but that bird never faltered, speeding onwards to clear the line of Scot's pines, and then dipping, gliding to safety in the valleys below.

"Well, I'll be . . ." I could not find words to express my disgust, annoyance, and shame., I felt like flinging my gun into a snowdrift, and cutting myself a stout ash-stick. Remus had emerged on to the ride by now, and stood looking at us, his tongue lolling to one side. I could swear he was laughing, enjoying some subtle canine joke at our expense.

"That's the end of our 'SGs', anyway," John reflected gloomily. "It'd be just our luck to have that darned deer get up in front of us now!"

We walked on, not talking, reprimanding ourselves for our lack of alertness, and bad marksmanship. Only Remus remained undaunted.

A hundred yards or so further on we came upon those cloven tracks again. They emerged out of the undergrowth in an unbroken line.

"I suppose we may as well follow to see where they lead to, having come so far," I lamented, lapsing once more into my mood of earlier that day.

"Only, if we *do* see it, don't for heaven's sake shoot at it, now that we've wasted our 'heavies'. We don't want to go home with a wounded deer on our consciences!"

On and on we trudged, still following that same tantalising, frustrating spoor. Bend after bend we rounded, and still it led on ahead of us, calling us on like a Pied Piper of the hills, whose call we were unable to resit. We were now on the south side of the hill, and way below us we could see the hamlet of Obley, the smoke from the chimneys drifting directly upwards, and then dispersing lazily in the frosty air.

"Another half mile, and we'll be back at the car," I commented, noticing that John was flagging somewhat also. "We've virtually done a circuit of the whole hill!"

We topped the last rise, the sheepfields on our left, my parked car in front of the gateway below us. Still that never-ending spoor led onwards.

We noticed a movement alongside the wire-netting fence in front of us, and, as we drew nearer, we saw that it was a man, dressed in the long brown smock and cap of a typical hill farmer, busily struggling to unroll some large mesh, and fasten it over a gaping hole which had rotted in the existing fence. He straightened up as we approached, and I immediately recognised the windbeaten complexion of the owner of this 90 acres or so of grazing land.

"Terrible cold, gentlemen," he called out in his high pitched, musical voice. "It'll freeze agin tonight, I know."

"More than likely," I replied, glad of the opportunity to rest for a few moments. I offered him my tobacco pouch, and he began stuffing the long strands into his small, well burnt briar, with a gnarled forefinger.

"Busy?" I asked, by way of conversation.

"So, so," he paused to strike a match, and puffed out clouds of blue smoke. "Once lambin' starts we shall be. Won't be more'n a couple o' weeks or so now. Lucky I spotted this break in the fence. Could've been tricky otherwise."

"Nasty hole," I commented, noting the jagged edges of the rotted wire-netting. "You could easily have had one or two sheep get out."

"Aye," he mused, pausing again to relight his pipe, the bowl of which was so crammed with my smoking mixture that it was almost impossible to draw upon it. "One did. Last night, or early this morning. Bin right round t'wood, and back in agin, through the same 'ole. Clever these sheep. Know where they're best off."

I just smiled, and breathed a sigh of relief.

DEERSTALKING

Deerstalking is a specialist sport, and those wishing to devote their efforts in this direction are advised to contact an experienced ghillie, and perhaps obtain permission to accompany him on one or two forays, so that they may understand the basic principles. Some skill with a rifle is necessary, for deer may not be shot legally with shot sizes smaller than SSG. In any case the risk of wounding with any shot size is high, and as such rifles of calibre .240 or larger must be used *accurately*.

In his previous book, *Gamekeeping and Shooting for Amateurs,* the author gave some advice on stalking procedure, but we must also bear in mind that there is always the possibility of meeting up with deer on a rough-shoot. Perhaps it will be one that has strayed from a local deer-park, although nowadays the spread of Sika throughout Britain is considerable.

The Sika stags have a silvery black coat, whilst the hinds are browny-grey.A fully-grown stag weighs almost as much as a fallow buck, and is not the paltry prize which it is often made out to be.

If you discover that deer are using your rough-shoot then you need to make careful preparations. You are best to go alone with your rifle, taking up a position close to where the deer have been reported feeding. It is necessary to sit still, refrain from smoking, and be patient. If a sound is heard, do not go to investigate. You won't creep up on a wary deer. *It is he who must come to you if you are going to be successful.*

The neck must be your target. Raise your weapon slowly. Any sudden movement is likely to be spotted. The head, contrary to popular opinion, is the place where much suffering is caused for the bullet can lodge in the jaw, and the creature will suffer for days before death finally brings release. Often a deer can be merely stunned by a head-shot, and as you walk towards it, it leaps up and runs away as if nothing has happened. But later, when it has successfully evaded you, its suffering will begin.

It is essential that one fully understands the seasons during which deer may be shot. Of course, if one arranges a deerstalking expedition, the stalker or ghillie will advise you, but it is the chance encounter, the foray after deer on the hill-shoot, where one must assume full responsibility, with which we are concerned in this book.

SEASONS.

RED DEER.

England and Wales.

1st August—30th April—Stags.

1st November—28/29th February—Hinds.

Scotland.

1st July—20th October—Stags.

21st October—15th February—Hinds.

FALLOW DEER.

England and Wales.

1st August—30th April—Bucks

1st November—28th February—Does.

Scotland.

1st August—30th April—Bucks.

21st October—15th February—Hinds.

181

As with every other type of shooting one must have conservation uppermost in mind. If a pair of deer stray on to your shoot it is often preferable to leave them alone, encourage them to remain, and there is always the possibility that they may breed there. However, complaints from farmers, once these animals begin damaging crops and forestry, may compel you to go out and stalk them.

If your shooting is leased from the Forestry Commission then consult your local Head or Beat Forester. The right to kill deer is excluded from most, if not all, of these leases, but even if the Forestry Commission insist on carrying out the culling of herds themselves you may well be allowed to accompany one of their marksmen. This is an opportunity not to be missed. You will learn how to shoot a deer with the greatest degree of accuracy and the minimum of suffering to the beast.

CHAPTER 12

Legends and Folklore

The hills abound with legends, some more localised than others. Each tract has its own particular one if you only take the trouble to talk to these hill people. Many of the crofters are superstitious folk, but generally they will recall the stories passed on down through the generations.

THE BLACK DOGS

The legend of the Black Dogs is a widespread one although comparatively few people have heard of it. It varies according to the locality, stretching as far down as Cornwall. I merely quote here the version attributed to the border hills which I know so well. Whether or not I actually encountered one of these spectral dogs, or whether there is a perfectly normal explanation for that which happened to me I shall probably never know. Perhaps it is better that way.

The Black Hill is seeped in legend and mythology, as indeed is any place which has been involved in the bloody wars between the English and the Welsh. The two castles which are in close proximity are Clun Castle and Hopton Castle, both of which were English fortifications. These ruins saw much border fighting in those far off days, and naturally both have their respective ghosts. However, I have my own particular spirits haunting the hill itself, and should I ever wish to organise a ghost-hunt I would not have to go beyond my own boundaries. Many of the locals give the Black Hill a wide berth after darkness has fallen, fearful of meeting with the terrible vengeance of the "Black Dogs". These dogs are supposed to roam the area, and its surroundings, in times when misfortunes are portending. Woe-betide he who is unfortunate enough to glimpse one, for ill will befall him. Legend has it that a sheep farmer was once confronted with one of these spectral dogs, centuries ago, whilst

12-1 "A Black Dog"—part of the mythology of the countryside.

(Drawing by Bob Sanders)

tending to his flock, just as darkness was falling. He struck at it with his shepherd's crook. As a result he was discovered in a state of terror and insanity the following morning, and he died a few days later.

I have only once had cause to give serious thought to these mythical canine stories. The incident in question happened one sweltering June afternoon. I had heard reports of a dog howling in my woods for nights on end, and one of my tenant farmers told me that his sheep were restless, and refused to graze close to the forestry fencing. Quite by chance I happened to pause for a well earned rest and a smoke in this particular place that day, and seating myself on a grassy bank, I proceeded to fill and light my pipe. Suddenly, my yellow labrador, Remus, gave a low growl, and his hackles began to rise. I noticed a movement in the undergrowth about forty yards away, and then I felt a shiver run up my spine as I caught a glimpse of the creature. I could only see the top half of it, for the rest was hidden by the bracken, but it was the most awful dog that it has ever been my lot to see. It was jet black in colour, and I judged it to be an Alsatian crossed with a collie. Its coat was covered in mange, and I could not help but remember the stories which the superstitious flockmasters had related to me. However, I could not allow such a beast to remain at large to the danger of sheep and game, so I had no hesitation in firing a charge of No. 5 shot directly at its head. The dog dropped, and for the first time in years Remus did not run in to shot. Instead he remained at heel, growling, but reluctant to move. I ran forward, eager to view the monstrosity which had just fallen to my gun, and then I pulled up in dismay, and I must admit, a strange feeling of apprehension came over me. There was no sign of the brute, nor even the slightest trace of blood or hairs! Remus refused to search the undergrowth, hanging back, still with that low growl in his throat.

I prefer to accept the logical explanation for that strange occurrence that sunny afternoon, and believe that I had shot over the top of the animal, and he had slunk off unhurt, or else had managed to escape, mortally wounded. Whatever the truth was, I never heard any more about it. The nocturnal dog was never again heard in the hills. The old shepherd, however, was inclined to favour the local legend. "You don't always meet up with these things in the dead of night, sir," he told me, puffing away at his old clay pipe. "They can come up on you in the woodland, in the middle of the afternoon, in bright sunlight, and then you may have to fight for your very life!"

Possibly it was a stray dog that had taken to the wild, living in some disused fox earth, and as such its removal was necessary to the safety of sheep and game alike. I leave the reader to draw his own conclusions.

It is a source of amazement to me that several of the hill legends have a seafaring origin, particularly a couple in my own locality where the nearest coastline is some eighty miles away.

CAPTAIN'S COPPICE

Captain's Coppice! The very name intrigues the visitor to this small acreage of woodland, with its crumbling stone wall boundary, and a background of steep sloping, thickly forested hillsides, part of, yet seemingly remote from, the hills beyond. It is a forgotten place of enchanting beauty, undiscovered by the hordes of weekend motorists during the summer months, due to its situation, and disregarded by its owners who saw fit to plant the once heather-covered adjoining hills with Scots pine and Norwegian spruce, and alter the landscape to their own artificial structure.

The Coppice remained untouched, allowed to weather the storms of progress as it had done for centuries, its giant oak, beech and chestnut trees maturing to such magnificence, some reaching their allotted lifespan, and then rotting back into the earth, others being denied this natural course of Nature by the sudden advent of an electric storm, leaving only hideous, blackened skeletons as reminders of their ever having existed at all.

The nearest inhabitants are a full mile away, living in farm cottages, and braving the elements throughout the long winter months. Captain's Coppice? Amazement is evident on their rugged, weatherbeaten faces when one broaches the subject. There's nothing to go there for, anyway, they explain, except perhaps to gather some dead wood to supplement their meagre fuel supplies. It hasn't altered since the days of their childhood. The trees have grown larger perhaps, and the undergrowth has become denser simply because nobody has bothered to brash it, but basically it is unchanged. Once somebody attempted to quarry for slate, but the rewards did not warrant the labour, so this enterprise was abandoned after only a few weeks. The Captain? The old farmer shook his head in bewilderment at my question. Yes, he'd heard his father speak of a seafaring man who had owned it way back in the time when his grandfather was a small boy. Rumour has it that this seaman had purchased it with his share of some treasure gained whilst at sea, possibly by piracy, but within a few months the owner of this

186

small wood was drowned in a sudden storm off Cape Horn. I wondered if by any chance the remnants of his steel bound chest of pieces-of-eight might be buried somewhere within the bounds of the Coppice! It is strange, indeed, that a man who spent the greater part of his life at sea should buy an isolated patch of woodland in the heart of the English countryside.

The first time I set foot in Captain's Coppice was in the late autumn. The rays of the sun filtered through the bare branches of the gigantic trees above me as I trod on a thick carpet of golden brown leaves. The very atmosphere was one of preparation for the bleak days which lay ahead, a sadness at the passing of summer, and the continuation of the desolation which had always been. I found the small disused slate quarry, now moss covered, and overgrown with weeds. As I approached it, a rabbit scurried up the far side, pausing to look back at me before disappearing into the safety of the surrounding clumps of dying bracken. He was obviously puzzled at my intrusion, not exactly afraid of me, but decided to take no chances. Perhaps it was the first time that he had set eyes on a human being.

Woodpigeons clattered noisily out of the treetops as I trespassed further. Obviously they preferred the tall roosting trees here to the stunted fir thickets on the slopes above. A grey squirrel darted up the massive trunk of a beech tree, and as I watched, it suddenly disappeared. Try as I did to spot him again, I could not, for instinct had taught him that his very survival lay in a combination of perfect camouflage and immobility.

As I progressed, it was obvious that the badgers were the true rulers of this small, compact kingdom. Their setts were in evidence in another clearing bordering on the fir plantations. I had expected to find Brock here, for badgers love old established woods, and, if allowed to remain there undisturbed, will use the same living quarters from one generation to the next.

In the topmost branches of an age-old fir tree I spied a huge nest, built firmly between two boughs and supported by the trunk. A raven's nest, deserted for the time being, but without a doubt, the parent birds, who are reputed to pair for life, would be returning to it again the following spring.

Having completed my tour of inspection of Captain's Coppice, I found myself back on the deserted roadside again. Apart from the occasional stick-gatherer, I was probably the only person to have intruded there for months, perhaps even years. Those who know it claim that it has nothing to offer. How wrong they all are, for I had discovered the Captain's buried treasure, not gold and silver, but peace and quietness, and a chance to appreciate life as it has gone on in our native countryside for hundreds and thousands of years. Somewhere in the distance, my ears caught the sound of a chainsaw, a sure sign that felling was taking place in one of the larger woods. A dull boom, which echoed ánd re-echoed throughout the hills. denoted blasting in one of the many quarries, only a mile or two distant. Captain's Coppice had been spared all this. But for how long?

THE SEAGULL POOL

Some time ago, whilst sitting on a grassy bank on the edge of my thickly wooded hill-shoot, I happened to notice the sunlight glinting on water, some three miles or so away, on the opposite range of hills, I merely made a mental note of the fact that there was water there, and promised myself that one day I would investigate it. Perhaps this was where the mallard came from which visited my own flight-pond at deepest dusk.

The weeks passed, and then, one day, when I happened to be occupying this place again, I was joined by a man and his wife, who had pulled their car off the country lane in order to picnic. During the course of conversation, I happened to remark upon the very fine pair of binoculars which they had with them, and was at once offered the chance to have a look through them. The magnification of the lenses was quite the most powerful I had ever experienced as I began focusing them on that distant, mysterious stretch of water. I caught my breath as the scene became so close that I might well have been standing on the water's edge. I estimated the pool to be something in the region of five acres, surrounded by reeds, and with a clump of willows growing in the middle, forming a minute island. It was quite enchanting, and as I studied the scene, I noted that the surface of the water was dotted with *seagulls!* Now, this would not be very remarkable in a suburban area, where there are ample refuse tips for these birds to scavenge, and recreation parks where people feed them, but to find them in numbers in the wilderness of these hills was, to say the least, most surprising. As I handed the binoculars back to their owner, I determined to visit this pool, as soon as possible, for I was greatly intrigued.

The following weekend, after relying upon my sense of direction through the narrow lanes, and then across a gated road, I suddenly came upon this pool, quite unexpectedly, resting in a hollow, only fifty yards from the main track. As I got out of the car, a flock of seagulls rose off the water, with raucous cries of indignation at this disturbance, and circled round, insulting me. I looked over the low hawthorn hedge which separated me from

188

the stretch of water, and found it to be exactly as I had seen it through those binoculars the previous week. The setting was so delightful that I paused to light my pipe and comtemplate awhile, watching the sun dip behind the distant horizon.

Suddenly, I was aware that a man was approaching in my direction, along the rutted cart-track. As he drew nearer, I saw that he had the lean, windswept look of a typical hill farmer. His complexion was tanned to the colour of mahogany, his clothes were patched, and protected by a piece of sacking which was tied around his waist with a length of binder-twine.

"You'm interested in the pool?" It was more of a statement of fact than a question. "Don't you'm know this is private land?"

"I'm sorry if I've trespassed," I replied, "But I was so intrigued by your pool, which, until today, I've only seen through binoculars from my shoot over yonder."

"No harm done." There was a different, more friendly, note in his voice now. "As for the pool, my father, and his'n before 'im, tried to drain it, but there's a dingle* seeps up out o' the ground. Never was this big, though, till two or three years back . . . when Uncle Reuben came to live 'ere."

"And who is Uncle Reuben?" I asked, sensing all the time that he merely wanted a lead to tell a yarn.

"Uncle Reuben," he began, "spent the whole of his bloomin' life at sea. A proper sefarin' man, 'e was. 'E was in the Merchant Navy up until they retired 'im—long after 'e should've retired! 'E allus used to come and stay 'ere when 'e had some leave. Never married. Anyway, when 'e found hisself wi' nowt to do, and time on 'is 'ands, 'e came 'ere. Visiting at first, and just stayed. 'E was the silly blighter who dammed this 'ere dingle up to make a proper pool. 'E said it'd make a good watering place for cattle in the dry weather. Truth was, 'e just liked water, and if 'e couldn't 'ave 'is blessed sea, then 'e thought e'd make hisself one!"

I tried to hide a smile, conjuring up a picture of an old seafaring man, gleefully watching his home-made lake slowly filling up, day by day.

"But the seagulls," I began, "surely it's strange that they should permanently inhabit a pool so far from civilisation?"

*A spring, but may also be a brook—see Chapter 13.

189

"Aye," The old farmer considered my question carefully, before replying. "They only came after Uncle Reuben died, though. Never seed in these here parts before then. It rained for a whole week after the funeral, day after day. That pool, with the dingle dammed up, filled up like you see it now. Then, about a fortnight later, a couple o' them gulls was on it one mornin'. They stayed, and others came to join 'em, as you can see. They stop 'ere all the time, breeding as well. Right now they're givin' us a bit o' stick. They don't like strangers one little bit—just like Uncle Reuben didn't, neither!"

I had much food for thought as I drove home that night. Why, indeed, did those seagulls frequent that isolated pool in the hills, unless, of course, they were the souls of long since departed seafaring friends of old Uncle Reuben, come to be near his last resting place? That is how I like to interpret the story, anyway.

QUICKSILVER'S GRAVE

There is one legend, which I feel I cannot omit from those already related, even though it concerns a tract of hill country some three hundred miles from those which I know so well, situated in the south-west corner of Scotland. Somehow this ridge of upland territory in the heart of the Solway Plain bears a similarity to my own shooting rights, rugged and sparse, yet luring me with the promise of the unexpected. For the past fifteen years I have holidayed there, a change of scenery yet incorporating a familiarity about it which is possibly the greatest appeal. Deep inside me I know that I am a 'hill man', and that I should have been born and bred in the type of terrain which I love so dearly. Nevertheless, it was on a mission of casual exploration that I came upon 'Quicksilver's Grave'.

The early morning September mists gradually dispersed on the hilltops as the first rays of the sun began to penetrate them, full of the promise of one of those early autumnal days. I paused on the rocky slope, and sat on a conveniently placed slab of rock from which I would be able to survey the whole countryside below me very shortly, once the remaining wisps of this swirling grey vapour had disappeared.

It was as I wandered over those hills on that enchanting morning, with Remus at my heels, that I made a discovery which has remained constantly in my memory ever since. I was walking through a long, narrow strip of coarse grass, interspersed with heather and gorse, hoping

190

for a shot at either grouse or a rabbit, when I came upon an upright stone slab. In spite of the fact that the undergrowth had almost obscured it from view, I had no difficulty in discerning the oblong mound adjoining it. There was no doubt in my mind that it was a grave, and I must confess that I felt slightly uneasy, not solely on account of this fact, but due to the immense size of it, for it was fully fifteen feet in length, and at least half that distance wide. Who, or what, was buried beneath it? I had a fleeting memory of a story my parents used to read to me regularly as an infant, entitled "Jack the Giant Killer!"

There was some lettering on the stone, but the elements had rendered it temporarily indecipherable, so with the aid of a large duster which I always carry in my bag for the purpose of drying off my dog at the end of a wet day, I set about cleaning it up. I worked for fully ten minutes, and then, as I stood back to admire my handiwork, I saw that the wording was now just legible. It read:

"QUICKSILVER—A GOOD HORSE AND A FAITHFUL SERVANT. DIED DECEMBER 1908. AGED 28 YEARS."

I lit my pipe, and seating myself on a nearby tussock of grass, I contemplated on my discovery. The sun had fully broken through by now, unravelling the panoramic view which lay below me, a fitting surrounding indeed for the last resting place of the faithful animal which was interred only a few feet away from me. The main factor which puzzled me was why the body of a horse had been transported up here. Whatever the reason, it would have taken at least half a dozen men to perform the task, and even then, without the assistance of a tractor or Land Rover, it would have presented problems, to say the least. Why had this particular site been chosen when there was ample space on more accessible ground below?

I carried on with my walk after some time, but my mind was beset with these mysteries, and I determined to unravel the story of Quicksilver, if at all possible. Surely no ordinary horse warranted a grave with such an elaborate stone, set in a place so apart from the rest of the everyday world that the very burial itself was a mammoth task.

However, my enquiries proved far more difficult than I had at first anticipated. On the very day of my discovery I called at the farmhouse on my way back to my hotel, primarily to thank the farmer for his kindness in allowing me to carry a gun on his land, and to offer him the hare which I had been fortunate enough to shoot, but also to see if he could throw any light on that grave situated on his furthermost boundary.

There I encountered my first stumbling block. This farmer did not even know of its existence!

"I've only been right up to the top a couple of times in the three years I've been here," he told me, "and on those occasions I was more interested in looking for a couple of stray ewes!"

I stopped to speak with his stockman as I collected my car from the muddy yard. Yes, he had been here in the days of the former owner, and he *did* know of Quicksilver's grave.

"I happened to come across it one day, 'bout five years ago," he replied in answer to my question. "Don't know what was buried in it, though. Couldn't make out the lettering, not that I'm much of a one for reading, anyhow. Nobody knew much about it, because there's been several owners of this place, over the years. Can't rightly say who owned it in 1908, though."

It was, indeed, a strange enquiry which I was conducting, for I could only pursue it annually, on the occasions of my autumnal holidays. Thus I spent a frustrating twelve months, constantly conjuring up a picture of a magnificent hunter, and its owner, heartbroken, when finally it passed on. I imagined a group of burly farmworkers, supervised by this man, hauling the body of the dead horse up the steep slope, an unenviable task, indeed.

It was three years before I finally unravelled the veil of mystery surrounding the legendary Quicksilver, and it came about when I had almost given up, but not forgotten, my quest. I was enjoying a quiet, after-dinner drink in the bar of the hotel, when I fell into conversation with a retired gamekeeper, a man who had once been in the service of the Duke of Norfolk, many years ago. I merely mentioned the lonely grave out of passing interest, never for one moment dreaming that he might in any way have been connected with the story.

"Aye, poor old Quicksilver," my companion sighed, sipping his glasses of beer and whiskey alternatively, and refusing to be hurried into his story in spite of my eagerness at the very mention of the horse's name. "My father remembered him well. The animal came from the estate, originally. A magnificent hunter, but suffered from some hereditary muscular trouble by the time he was ten. It was touch and go whether he was destroyed or not, but one of the tenant farmers on the estate, an ardent horse-lover, begged him off the agent. Naturally, the agent was only too pleased to pension the crippled beast off, and so the farmer came and fetched him one Sunday morning. He was a good man, that farmer, and he really worked on Quicksilver. The vet practically lived there for the first few months. I won't go as far as to say that they actually cured him, but suffice to say he enjoyed a good five year's hunting before they pensioned him off, and gave him the freedom of the place. He wandered just where he liked, but his favourite place was that rocky hilltop behind the farm. He'd stand there for hours on end, silhouetted against the skyline like a stone statue, just content to be alive, and grateful to the man who'd given him all this."

I thought I detected a mistiness in his eyes as he finished his story, but perhaps it was my own vision which became slightly blurred.

"He died up there, you know," the old keeper concluded. "A fitting place, indeed, for such a magnificent animal to end his days. They went out to look for him in the snow, and found him lying up there in his favourite place. It would have been almost impossible to have got him down, so they set to with pick-axes and shovels, and buried him up there. A few months later Quicksilver's owner had a stone erected to him, and it's still there to this day."

So that was it. At last I had pieced together the story of that faithful horse, an animal who had been grateful for just being allowed to live in peace for eighteen years on borrowed time. I am glad that I had taken the trouble to unravel these events which had taken place over seventy years ago, and I shall try and find time to go and visit that lonely grave each autumn. I shall probably be his only visitor from one year to the next.

The legends of our hills are many. These are but a few which I have come across personally. There is something about this type of country which inspires them, an embracing atmosphere which is pregnant with memories of days long gone.

CHAPTER 13

The Unexpected: the Lure of the Hills

As stated elsewhere in this book, one can never predict the quality of a day's shooting. Unlike lowland keepered estates where fairly consistent averages are maintained, it is totally different in the hills. I have long since ceased to welcome 'ideal' conditions. Rarely does one's quarry conform to pattern. Pigeons flight in on inexplicable flight-lines when a study of wind direction takes one to a totally 'blank' stand. Pheasants are flushed from unpredictable places, woodcock suddenly appear in numbers, here one day, gone the next. One never knows what to expect.

Sometimes one neglects a particular area for long spells, regarding the time and effort better spent in more worthwhile places. I did hust this on my own shoot, regarding the steep climb down to 'The Dingle' to be hardly worth the odd pigeon or rabbit which it had produced on previous occasions. I am still regretting those seasons when I ignored this place.

'The Dingle' owes its name to the fact that a small brook runs between two hills. The locals never even think of it as a valley, but that is just what it is, two steep hills separated by this narrow valley which meanders out on to the sloping grazing fields at the far end. The one hill consists solely of an impenetrable Forestry Commission thicket, the other a few larch trees, a clump of hawthorn bushes, and a cattle-drink where the stream widens out. Perhaps a flockmaster goes there from time to time in search of a missing sheep, but mostly it is deserted apart from the wildlife of these border hills. Buzzards soar in the hope of an odd rabbit, a pair of ravens favour the giant larches, and a jay seems to spend its life dedicated to warning its few colleagues of the wild should Man decide to descend the steep track from the narrow road several hundred feet above.

Possibly a decade ago I knew the Dingle better than most, for the one hill incorporated the furthermost boundary of my shooting rights in these lonely border hills. I signed my lease a couple of years after it was first planted,

195

and watched the trees grow up. In the early days it was possible to beat out the newly furrowed slope, provided that one stepped carefully, for it would have been only too easy to break an ankle. Possibly the descent was more treacherous than the return journey, but however one viewed it, it was a test of one's physical fitness. Rarely did the exercise reap a sporting reward, and only once can I remember having to tackle the return climb whilst weighed down with a hare in my game-bag. I believe that I had been lured down there by the calling of a cock pheasant, but I never managed to find him.

Then the trees began to grow, their branches impeding one's progress, but worst of all was the gorse which grew in abundance in any place where the sunlight penetrated. I decided that this part of my shoot was simply a wasted acreage, and concentrated on the more lucrative parts of the hills above. The Dingle remained unkeepered and unshot.

Something which had always puzzled me was the ownership of the actual floor of the valley. The one hillside was forestry, the other part of a hill farm, but nobody laid claim to that twenty yards wide strip of land which ran between. Perhaps it was a case of boundaries which had not quite adjoined, I decided.

Then one day I experienced a desire to renew my acquaintance with this part of my shoot again. Not wishing to fight my way down to the Dingle through the thickly planted spruce, I obtained permission from the farmer opposite for access from his side. He claimed that the rabbits 'in the forestry' were on the increase, and was only too pleased for my shooting partner and myself to attempt to reduce their numbers.

So Bob and I returned to the Dingle after an absence of practically a decade. The hoar frost glinted in the bright sunshine like tinsel on rows of Christmas trees, and a buzzard soared hopefully above us in a cloudless blue sky. Even the dogs seemed to share our enthusiasm for revisiting an old haunt although their optimism for the more practical side of the foray was greater than ours. Even so, I had evolved a plan of action the night before. I would walk on ahead as far as the end of the valley, and take up a stance beyond the cattle-drink, whilst Bob would work the whole length of the stream towards me. There was no wind, whatsoever, and it was reasonable to assume that anything put up by the dogs, and missed by him, would head towards me.

I settled down comfortably and lit my pipe. The descent had made me warm, and I was grateful for the rest. That 'rest' lasted precisely five minutes. My first intimation that there was a prospect of some sport was a double

196

report from Bob, and a solitary woodcock jerking and weaving its way towards me. I missed with my first barrel but somehow succeeded in bringing it down on the opposite bank of the stream with my second. As I prepared to wade the shallow gushing water to retrieve it, a second 'cock bore down upon me. My hurried late shot was a mere salute as it disappeared round the bend behind me. As I turned to watch its departure a sudden movement caught my eye. Something grey emerged from the frosty golden bracken and hopped towards the nearest forestry fence. Another shot, and I had a rabbit and a woodcock in the bag. Any moment now I would see Bob coming round the bend in the stream. I could already hear the dogs working. Well, it had certainly been worth it.

Bob joined me, and we stood talking, delighted with the way things had turned out. Our guns rested against the fence, and both labradors sniffed through the bracken and gorse around us. So pleased were we with that which in the eyes of others would have seemed meagre results for much endeavour, that we failed to notice the tails of the two labradors wagging fiercely. Seconds later our tranquility was shattered as a cock pheasant burst from cover, red and gold plumage scintillating in the morning sunlight as it gained height, levelled out, and with its final taunting 'cock-up' ringing in our ears, disappeared from view amongst the thorn bushes halfway up the opposite hillside.

Bob and I looked at each other. The wily old bird, perhaps a direct descendant of the one which had once lured me down the Dingle all of ten years ago, had beaten us. It had lain within a few yards of me as I had fired at woodcock and rabbit, and had awaited its chance. Perhaps one day our paths would cross again, and then the bird might not be so fortunate. In the meantime, though, I wished it well, and hoped that it would be as successful in eluding Reynard.

The woodcock and the rabbit in my game-bag, we began the steep climb back up the slope, leaving behind us the Dingle and its secrets of nature. High above us that buzzard still soared, wheeling, gliding, it ragged moth-like wings gracefully propelling it back and forth above this tiny remote valley. Possibly only this large hawk knew all that went on down there. We had merely infiltrated for a very short time.

One can spend a lifetime in the hills, but each day brings forth something new. One never stops learning. Always there is a fresh challenge to the sportman in upland territory. And it has to be met, win or lose.

Index